100 things you must know

English

Imelda Pilgrim, Brian Conroy, Lorna Smith

Published by BBC Educational Publishing, BBC White City, 201 Wood Lane, London W12 7TS

First published 2000

© Imelda Pilgrim, Brian Conroy, Lorna Smith/BBC Worldwide (Educational Publishing), 2000

Colour reproduction, Printed and bound in England by Ebenezer Baylis

To place an order, please telephone Customer Services on 01937 541001 (Monday–Friday 0800–1800) or write to BBC Educational Publishing, PO Box 234, Wetherby, West Yorkshire LS23 7EU.

Visit the BBC Education website at http://www.bbc.co.uk/education

Contents

Introduction

About GCSE BITESIZE

- GCSE BITESIZE is a revision service designed to help you achieve success in your exams with **books, television programmes** and a website at **www.bbc.co.uk/education/revision.**

- It's called BITESIZE because it breaks revision into bitesize chunks to make it easier to learn.

How to use this book

- This book explains and tests the **100 Things You Must Know** to succeed in GCSE English. It provides:
  - skills or key information you need for each of the 100 topics in the 'Know the facts' sections
  - questions to test your understanding in the 'Test yourself' sections.

- Use this book to check your understanding of GCSE English. If you can prove to yourself that you're confident with these key ideas you'll know that you're on track with your learning.

- You can use this book to test yourself:
  - during your GCSE course
  - at the end of the course, while revising.

- As you revise you can use *100 Things You Must Know* in several ways:
  - as a summary of the key information on each of the 100 key topics to help you revise those areas
  - to check your revision progress: test yourself to see which topics you're confident with
  - as a way to keep track and plan your time: you can aim to check and test a set number of topics each time you revise, knowing how many you need to cover in total and how much time you've got.

More GCSE Bitesize revision materials

There's nothing like variety for making revision more interesting, and covering a topic from several different angles is an ideal way to make it stick in your head. There are lots of GCSE Bitesize Revision materials in different media, so take your choice and make learning enjoyable.

GCSE Bitesize Revision: English is a **book** which contains the key information and skills you need to revise, plus lots of tips and practice questions to help you improve your results. GCSE Bitesize Revision: English book ISBN: 0 563 46118 7.

The GCSE Bitesize Revision: English **CD-ROM** takes you through your exam texts with a helpful commentary on the important things you should know and lots of practice questions, with answers, so you can test yourself. CD-ROM ISBN: 0 563 54281 0.

The GCSE Bitesize Revision: English **website** provides even more text extracts and the opportunity to practise your reading and writing skills. Website address: **www.bbc.co.uk/education/revision.**

About GCSE

During the GCSE English course, you will be asked to do a number of writing tasks. These include:

- writing to explore, persuade and advise

- writing to inform, explain and describe

- writing to analyse, review and comment.

Where you do each type of writing depends on the examination specification (syllabus) you are following. Some of the topics may be covered in coursework and some may be tested in an exam. You should find out from your teacher which ones you need to revise for the exam.

BITESIZE concentrates on the essentials, but it doesn't cover everything you need to know, or all the things you'll need to be able to do. However, there are some skills you will need whatever type of writing you are doing.
These are:

1. Planning your work

This is vitally important, because it shows the examiner that you have thought through the whole piece, rather than just making it up as you go along. The person who marks your work will be looking for evidence that your writing is deliberate. A plan shows that you have thought about:

- your introduction and conclusion

- what each paragraph will be about

- the shape of the writing – the order of your paragraphs.

2. Checking your work

When you have finished writing, you must go back and check everything. Look at how your sentences work – are there some which could be clearer? Think about ways you could make your writing more effective by adding or deleting a few words. Look for common spelling and punctuation mistakes – try to be aware of those you often make.

We hope you enjoy working with GCSE BITESIZE English *100 Things You Must Know.*

Good Luck!

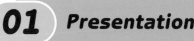

01 Presentation

Know the facts ⏳

First impressions count and one of the first things an examiner will notice when assessing your writing is your presentation. Presentation is assessed on handwriting and spelling. It may sound obvious but, in an exam, the examiner must be able to read your handwriting. The more difficulty he or she has in reading your writing the less likely he or she is to feel positive about your paper.

Here are some of the criticisms made about students' handwriting:

- Too large and loopy
- Letters not clearly defined
- No distinction between heights of letters
- Letters too small
- Letters slanted in different directions
- Blotchy writing

You probably know by now if you have a problem with your handwriting. Your teacher, or a friend, may have spoken to you about it. Perhaps there is only a problem when you are writing under pressure in an exam. Perhaps you simply need to invest in a better pen!

Test yourself ⏳

Write the words of a song that you know. Now ask yourself:

(a) Are the letters clearly formed?

(b) Are the letters an appropriate size?

(c) Can all the words be read without effort?

(d) Does it look reasonably tidy?

Double check by asking a parent or friend to assess your handwriting by answering the same questions. Focus on the area that needs improvement.

02 Spelling simple words

Know the facts ⏳

- Many students think they are poor spellers but most students spell most words correctly most of the time. Problems arise with simple words that are used often.

There are seven spelling errors in the following passage. Can you find them? What are the correct spellings?

> I have one main ambition in life and it's based on my intrest in fashion. I hope to make it in the fashion buisness, though I allready know it's not going to be easy. I like to shop. That's where it all started. I would go into town every Saturday with my freinds and we'd spend hours looking in shop windows and trying on diffrent cloths. None of us had allot of money but we all liked to dream of the day when we could buy everything we wanted.

- The most common mistakes are made with words that are used often. Make sure you know the difference between these commonly-used words that sound the same but have a different meaning. Use a dictionary if you are not sure.

| they're | there | their |
| we're | were | where |

- In your English exams you are assessed on the accuracy of your spelling. You need to:
  - be aware of words you often misspell
  - learn how to spell those words correctly.

Test yourself ⏳

Look through your English exercise books and list the words you have spelled incorrectly. Write the correct spelling of all these words.

> Learn the words you have difficulty spelling by using one or all of the following techniques:
>
> - Form a visual pattern of the word in your mind.
> - Say the word, pronouncing it clearly.
> - Cover the word and practise writing it correctly.

Know the facts

- Many words are made up of different parts. The main part of a word is called the stem.

- **Prefixes** are attached to the beginning of a word and alter its meaning, for example:

Prefix	Stem	Word
dis	agree	disagree
un	necessary	unnecessary
pre	historic	prehistoric
mis	adventure	misadventure
im	possible	impossible
in	direct	indirect

- **Suffixes** are added to the end of a word. They also alter the meaning of the word, for example:

Stem	Suffix	Word
entertain	ment	entertainment
triumph	ant	triumphant
courage	ous	courageous
hope	fully	hopefully
push	ing	pushing
kind	ness	kindness

- The English language uses many other prefixes and suffixes. Awareness of the wide range of prefixes and suffixes used will help you to spell words more accurately.

Test yourself

1 What prefixes could be attached to these words?

carry	connect	dependent	direct
helpful	kind	mature	pulse
sincere			

2 What suffixes could be attached to these words?

expect	general	grace	move
perform	persist	point	short
thank	walk		

Know the facts

When we speak we do not need to include punctuation. At the end of a sentence we don't say 'full stop'. There is no need to. We naturally pause to make sense of what we are saying for the benefit of our listener. If we are asking a question we don't need to say 'question mark' at the end of the sentence. We naturally raise the pitch of our voice so that it is obvious we are asking a question.

When you write, the reader cannot hear the changes in the tone of your voice and the pauses you make. That is why you need to use punctuation. It is the way you make your meaning clear to your reader.

- Here are some of the punctuation marks that you need to know and use:

capital letter	C
full stop	.
question mark	?
exclamation mark	!
comma	,

Test yourself

1 Which punctuation mark indicates the following?

(a) surprise, anger, warning or humour

(b) a pause within a sentence

(c) the end of a complete statement

(d) the start of a sentence or a name

(e) a question has been asked

2 Read the following passage and decide where you need to place punctuation marks.

have you understood this page so far just to recap if you don't use punctuation then your words become very difficult to follow the reader becomes confused and your writing becomes less effective you must punctuate your writing if you want your reader to understand what you have written simple

01

02

03

04

Know the facts

There are some rules you can learn that affect a lot of words.

Making plurals

• Usually:	just add s	e.g.	computer	computer<u>s</u>
			school	school<u>s</u>
• Words that end in:				
s, x, sh, ch	add es	e.g.	loss	loss<u>es</u>
			tax	tax<u>es</u>
			fish	fish<u>es</u>
			church	church<u>es</u>
			fox	fox<u>es</u>
• Words that end in:				
a vowel + y	add s	e.g.	day	day<u>s</u>
a consonant + y	cut off y and add ies			
		e.g.	lady	lad<u>ies</u>
• Words that end in:				
f or fe	cut off f/fe and add ves			
		e.g.	wolf	wol<u>ves</u>
			knife	kni<u>ves</u>
• Words that end in:				
o	add s	e.g.	zoo	zoo<u>s</u>

Changing verb endings

- Usually just add *ing* or *ed* to the stem of the word, for example:

  walk   walk<u>ing</u>   walk<u>ed</u>

- If the verb already ends in *e* just add *d*, for example:

  love   love<u>d</u>

- If the verb has one syllable, a long vowel and ends with *e*, cut off the *e* and add *ing*, for example:

  like   lik<u>ing</u>

- If the verb ends in a consonant + *y*, change the *y* to *i* before adding *ed*, for example:

  try   tr<u>ied</u>

- If the verb has one syllable, a short vowel and ends in a single consonant, double the consonant and add the ending, for example:

  bat   bat<u>ting</u>   bat<u>ted</u>

Exceptions

- There are nearly always exceptions to the rules in English. Some words have irregular plurals, for example *child – children, potato – potatoes*. Learn these exceptions as you come across them.

Test yourself

1 Write the plurals to the following words.

bike	car	life	man
baby	box	family	princess
stitch	thief	sheep	match

2 Add *ed* or *d* to the following words, making any other necessary changes.

hurry	tip	cry	laugh
call	hate	push	empty
spot	lie	stop	fry

Know the facts

There are a number of other punctuation marks you need to know and use.

Apostrophes replace the missing letters when:
- words are shortened or contracted, for example:

  do not becomes *don't*

  I have becomes *I've*

- showing that something belongs to something or somebody, for example:

  the bag belonging to Sarah becomes *Sarah's bag*

  the mother of John becomes *John's mother*

Colons
- introduce a list, a quotation, a piece of speech or a question, for example:

  When going on holiday remember: lock the doors, leave a note for the milkman and make sure you've got your passport.

Semi-colons
- create a pause in a sentence where a comma would be too weak and a full stop would be too strong, for example:

  The holiday was marvellous; there were blue skies and sunshine every day.

Inverted commas or quotation marks
- show that a word or group of words is quoted from another text, for example:

  Romeo is so moved by the sight of Juliet he claims that she 'doth teach the torches to burn bright'.

- show words that are actually spoken, for example:

  'Where are you going?' asked Kate, curiously.

  'Just into town', replied her daughter, turning to avoid her mother's gaze.

Test yourself

Some punctuation is missing from the following passage. Make the appropriate corrections.

> The childrens father walked slowly along the beach. He didnt want to give up the search just yet. On the horizon the sun was closing over the waters edge the day was almost ended. As he walked he thought of all the things that had gone wrong over the past week the lost luggage, the dirty hotel room, the rain and now this. His thoughts were disturbed by shouts in the distance.
>
> Over here. Theres something over here.
>
> Now he was running running in the direction of the voices.

05

06

07 Using a wide range of words

Know the facts 🕮

* Some GCSE students are still using the same vocabulary range that they used in primary school. Read this extract in which a student describes his ideal home.

> The living room would have a lot of armchairs and big settees. It would have a massive television which had good sound and pictures. There would be a fire in every room for winter to keep it nice and warm. The dining room would have a big table for twenty people so that at Christmas I could have a big family dinner.

* The writing is clear and accurate but the words used are relatively simple. He probably knew and used the same words when he was eleven. Compare it to this extract on the same subject.

> The kitchen, the centre of the house in every way, would always be warm, its gentle, rosy glow seeping out and spreading through the house. The stove would always generate fantastic smells, some familiar, age-old, some exotically different and enticing. Next to the stove a lazy cat would cosily pass its time, gently drifting in and out of hazy sleep, moved only by the smell of fish and a tickle behind the ear.

* This writing uses more sophisticated words such as *seeping, generate, exotically* and *enticing*. The student is showing that he knows a wide range of words from which he can choose appropriate ones. You need to show your examiner that you have access to a wide vocabulary range.

Test yourself 🕮

Rewrite these sentences, showing that you have a wide vocabulary. The first one has been done for you.

1 When the light had gone, the children came out of their houses.

   When the last rays of light had disappeared, the children crept stealthily from their houses.

2 The parcel was placed in the safe and the safe was locked.

3 The dining hall was full of noisy schoolchildren.

4 There were pictures on the walls and carpets on the floor.

08 Adjectives

Know the facts 🕮

* An **adjective** is a word that is used to tell the reader more about the noun.

* Adjectives can come before the noun, for example:

   a <u>spectacular</u> event   the <u>proud</u> parents

   or after the noun, for example:

   the event is <u>spectacular</u>   the parents are <u>proud</u>

* You can use adjectives together to create a more detailed picture, for example:

   The <u>weary</u>, <u>old</u> man turned his <u>tired</u>, <u>gentle</u> gaze on me, his <u>kindly</u> eyes reflecting memories of <u>happier</u> times gone by.

* Don't overdo them though, as in this example:

   The <u>cheerful</u>, <u>happy</u>, <u>young</u> lady looked out on the <u>bright blue</u> skies and the <u>stunning</u>, <u>yellow</u> sunshine and smiled a <u>brilliant</u>, <u>gleaming</u> <u>smile</u>.

* Adjectives create mood and atmosphere. Read these two sentences. The adjectives are underlined.

   The chair he was sitting in was <u>tattered</u> and <u>torn</u>, while the room itself was <u>dark</u> and <u>dusty</u> with a few <u>chipped</u> ornaments on the windowsill and some <u>faded</u> photographs on the walls.

   The chair he was sitting in was <u>crisp</u> and <u>cheerful</u>, while the room itself was <u>bright</u> and <u>clean</u> with a few <u>polished</u> ornaments on the windowsill and some <u>treasured</u> photographs on the wall.

* See how the adjectives create two very different rooms.

Test yourself 🕮

1 Underline the adjectives in this passage:

> The playground was silent. Vicious eyes followed him from behind the drawn blinds. Spiteful fingers pointed at him. Invisible faces mouthed cruel words. He knew they were there but he didn't turn to look. He had other, more important things, on his mind.

2 Write two or three sentences describing a beach:

   (a) in the daytime   (b) at night.

Aim to create two very different moods by your use of adjectives. You could choose adjectives from this list:

balmy, boisterous, calm, cool, colourful, gentle, hectic, lively, mysterious, peaceful, radiant, subdued, tranquil

 **Verbs**

Know the facts

- A **verb** is a word which is used to describe:
  - actions and movement, for example:
    She <u>stumbled</u> down the hillside.
  - feelings and thoughts, for example:
    She <u>hurt</u> her leg.

- There are also parts of the verbs 'to have' and 'to be' which can be used on their own or with other verbs, for example:

  We <u>have</u> six miles left to go.

  We <u>are</u> <u>travelling</u> towards the coast.

- Choose your verbs carefully so that they capture your ideas precisely. There is a huge range of verbs from which to choose. Think, for example, about all the verbs that show how somebody can say something:

  > S/he ... <u>bawled</u> bellowed cried exclaimed grumbled grunted moaned muttered screamed shouted snarled stuttered roared whimpered whispered yelled and so on.

- Choose the verb best suited to the action or feeling you are describing.

Test yourself

1 Rewrite these sentences using different combinations of verbs to create different effects.

(a) He walked (ran shuffled strode) towards the door, went (barged passed sidled) through it and closed (bolted nudged slammed) it behind him.

(b) The wind blew (rustled whispered whistled) through the trees, moving (shuffling twisting whirling) the leaves and stirring (agitating disturbing skimming) the pond water.

2 Think of alternative verbs to use in these sentences.

(a) When Sam <u>kicked</u> the ball, it <u>hit</u> the goalpost and <u>bounced</u> into the crowd.

(b) The office block <u>was</u> <u>built</u> in the centre of town, although many people <u>had</u> <u>wanted</u> it elsewhere.

10 **Adverbs**

Know the facts

- **Adverbs** are used to describe the ways things are done or felt or thought, for example:

  They shopped <u>determinedly</u>.

  His foot ached <u>dreadfully</u>.

  She worried <u>ceaselessly</u>.

- Adverbs work with the verb, answering questions about it, for example:

  He smiled. How did he smile? He smiled <u>slyly</u>.

  She drove. Which way did she drive? She drove <u>forwards</u>.

  They went to school. When did they go to school? They went to school <u>earlier</u>.

Pick out the adverbs in the following passage.

> The waves rolled lazily inwards, gently dropping shells and debris onto the sandy shore. Silently, they invaded the deserted beach, reaching forwards to the distant line of sand dunes.

- Many adverbs are formed by adding the suffix *-ly* to adjectives, for example:

  The boy was <u>slow</u>. (adjective)

  The boy moved <u>slowly</u>. (adverb)

  The moon is <u>bright</u> tonight. (adjective)

  The moon is shining <u>brightly</u> tonight. (adverb)

- You can improve the quality of your writing by thinking carefully about the adverbs you use, and ensuring you have a wide range of adverbs from which to choose.

Test yourself

1 Form adverbs from the following adjectives.

cold	dangerous	mischievous	mysterious
restless	thoughtful	quick	angry

2 Write a description of a child in a playground. Use adverbs to convey the way the child moves, plays, feels and talks.

11 Simile and metaphor

Know the facts

- The term **imagery** is applied to particular kinds of descriptive language. Two forms of imagery often used by writers are similes and metaphors.

- In a **simile** a writer compares something to something else, for example:

  The moon hung in the sky like a golden candle.

  Here the moon is compared to a golden candle.

- In a **metaphor** a writer says it actually **is** something else, for example:

  The sun shone brightly, a golden globe of glittering light.

  Here the sun is described as actually **being a** golden globe.

- Similes and metaphors have similar effects. They both help to create a clearer picture for the reader.

- The occasional use of simile and metaphor will show your examiner that you can use language effectively.

Test yourself

1 Think about the ways the writer uses metaphor and simile in the following examples. How do they help to convey:

   (a) the feelings of a hitchhiker?

   (b) the appearance of a place?

> (a) I could see a car or truck on the horizon I would become filled with expectation. Twenty minutes and seventeen bitter rejections later, I was beginning to feel a little low. No doubt about it, I was on the ropes. Actually I was on the canvas with the count having reached about six.
>
> (b) The terrain was rocky and sparsely covered with gorse, and it was peppered with little white houses dotted around as if a giant had dropped them like confetti from the sky.
>
> *Round Ireland with a Fridge* by Tony Hawks

2 Create your own metaphors/similes to describe:

   (a) an angry and out-of-control toddler

   (b) an isolated cottage on a hillside.

12 Types of sentence structures

Know the facts

There are three main types of sentence:

- **Simple sentences** are the first kind of sentences you learn to write. They communicate one idea, for example:

  The bus was late.

- **Compound sentences** link two or more simple sentences by using words such as *and*, *but*, *so* and *or*. These linking words are called conjunctions, for example:

  The bus was late so we walked home.

- **Complex sentences** communicate more than one idea by using two or more clauses, usually separated by commas, for example:

  The bus was late, probably because of the heavy snowfall, so we walked home.

Identify the different types of sentences used here.

> The room was full. Inside, bodies heaved and shook to the sound of the music. Nobody heard the boy as he entered the room. Nobody saw him until it was too late.

- Sentences may be short:

  He turned and saw her dancing.

  or quite long:

  He turned, nervously fingering his jacket, and saw her, the girl who only hours before had told him she would love him forever, dancing with another man.

- One is not necessarily better than the other but they are different. Short sentences can be used to build up a pacy rhythm and to create tension and impact.

- The second sentence gives a lot more detail. You will often be asked to give detail in your writing.

Test yourself

Using the example above to help you, develop your own complex sentences from the following.

1 The children ran through the gates.

2 The picture hung in the attic.

3 The plane rose into the sky.

13 **Thinking about sentence forms**

Know the facts

Writers choose their sentence forms carefully to create particular effects. Here are some examples of how sentence forms can be adapted to create particular effects:

- **Rhetorical question**, for example:

  Have you seen our prices?

By asking a direct question the writer involves the reader.

- **Exclamation**, for example:

  It's a disgrace!

The use of the exclamation mark implies strong feeling like shock or horror. It emphasises a particular point.

- **Group of three**, for example:

  Those suffering from AIDS in Africa have no families to turn to (1), no money to buy drugs (2) and no place to go to die (3).

The sequence of three connected points emphasises the issues.

- **Repetition**, for example:

  The choices you make now could change your future, change your life.

The repetition of particular words and phrases gives them extra impact.

- **Short sentence**, for example:

  I thought it would be easy to sort things out later. I was wrong.

The short sentence helps to emphasise an important point. It sometimes acts as a warning to the reader.

Test yourself

1 Read the passage and identify the following features.

(a) group of three

(b) rhetorical question

(c) use of repetition

(d) short sentence

> Kathy left school immediately after her GCSEs. She had no job to go to but at first she wasn't too worried. She had her brains, her confidence and three hundred pounds in her pocket. Why should she worry? Two months later she wasn't so confident; two months later she still had her brains but her money had disappeared along with her confidence. She didn't know which way to turn. She was frightened.

11

12

13

14 Using sentence forms for effect

Know the facts

- One thing an examiner will look for is your ability to use a range of sentence forms for effect.

Read the following examples. The first is taken from the writing of a D-grade candidate. The second is taken from the writing of an A-grade candidate.

> When it finally came down to it I did not have many choices to make. I had to take subjects like Maths and English. I also had to take Science though I could choose between a shorter or a longer course. I chose German as my modern language because I liked it better than French. I then had a free choice of subjects and I chose History and Geography as I enjoyed these most and I felt I could do well in them.
>
> Panicked and shocked I ran out of the room, not knowing what to do. What could I do? Who should I tell? Where should I go? Thoughts were circling my brain at high speed. I should already be at the charity dinner but was neither hungry nor, any longer, motivated by the wish to help others. In three short minutes my life had turned upside down. Nothing would ever be the same again. I was devastated.

- Notice how skilled the A-grade candidate is in using a range of sentence forms. Whilst the D-grade candidate's sentences are clearly formed they are very repetitive with most of them starting with *I*.

- The A-grade candidate's sentences are varied and there is a clear awareness of an audience with the use of rhetorical questions, in a group of three. The short sentence at the end of the paragraph is used for effect to emphasise the strength of the emotion.

Test yourself

Write a paragraph in which you explain your option choices. Use a range of sentence structures and vary your sentence openings. The aim is to make your writing lively and interesting for the reader.

15 Dealing with tenses

Know the facts

- Actions can happen in the present, the past or the future. You can use different tenses of a verb to show this. English has many different ways of expressing tenses. Look at the following.

I will be talking	I talk	I shall talk
I talked	I have talked	I will talk
I had talked	I was talking	
I am talking	I will have talked	

Which phrases are in the present tense? The past? The future?

- Certain kinds of writing require a particular tense:
  - A newspaper report usually describes things after they have happened and uses the past tense.
  - A school report, however, usually describes how a pupil is working at the time and is often written in the present tense.
  - A horoscope predicts what will happen in the future and requires the future tense.

- Stories can be written in the present, future or past tense or a mixture of all three. Most often, however, they are written in the past.

- A book or film review is often written in the present tense.

- It is important in your writing that:
  - you are consistent in your use of tense
  - you show control over the different ways of expressing tense
  - you know when to use which tense.

Test yourself

1 Write a horoscope for a friend, predicting what the next month will bring.

2 Write a review of a film or television programme you have seen recently.

16 Paragraphing for organisation

Know the facts

Just as we organise words into sentences, so sentences are organised into paragraphs.

- A **paragraph** is one of a number of blocks into which a text is subdivided. This helps the reader to follow the text more easily than if it were written in one solid block.

- In handwritten texts a paragraph is usually marked by the beginning of a new line and the indention of the first word.

- In printed texts a new paragraph may also be indicated by an increased space between lines.

- Each paragraph usually contains a series of sentences on the same topic. So, for example, if you were writing about your life at school you might choose to write four distinct paragraphs, each dealing with a different aspect of school life.

Paragraph 1	describing the school buildings and grounds
Paragraph 2	explaining which subjects you take
Paragraph 3	assessing the importance of friends at school
Paragraph 4	weighing up the benefits and disadvantages of school life

- If you use paragraphs well you can guide your reader through your subject and get your ideas across more effectively.

Test yourself

Make paragraph plans for two of the following subjects.

(a) holidays

(b) an evening with the family

(c) good and bad neighbours

Each paragraph plan should contain the outline for at least four distinct paragraphs.

17 Writing for purpose

Know the facts

- The purpose of a piece of writing is the reason for which it has been written. It may have been written to inform, advise, entertain, review or persuade. What is the purpose of this piece of writing?

> **End of Days (18)**
>
> **Stars:** Arnold Schwarzeneggar
>
> **Plot:** Arnie's back! This time as down-and-out ex-cop Jericho, who must pit his wits against evil Satan (Gabriel Byrne) to stop him taking over the world. Explosive, in-yer-face action and Byrne is spookily excellent as the Devil.
>
> **Released:** June 19
>
> *More* 14–27 June 2000

- A writer may well have more than one purpose in mind, for example the writer of a charity letter may be aiming to:

  - inform people of the work of the charity
  - raise funds for the charity.

- When starting a writing task the first thing you need to work out is your purpose. Why are you writing? What are you hoping to achieve?

Test yourself

Read the following writing tasks. For each one work out and write down the purpose or purposes.

(a) A company has just introduced a new hair product into its hair care range. It wants the public to know about the product and to buy it. Write the text for an advertisement for this product.

(b) You have just read an article in a magazine about the use of animals in experiments. Write a letter to the magazine arguing your point of view.

(c) Describe a scientific experiment, explaining the results you got and their significance.

(d) Your Head of Year is keen to improve the image of your year group. Write a report for your School Governors about a recent sporting event at school which was mainly organised by Year 11 pupils.

14

15

16

17

Know the facts

Your examiner will be assessing whether you are in control of your material and able to plan for paragraphing.

- Good paragraphing organises the material coherently and makes fluent links between one paragraph and the next.

- Sometimes a single sentence paragraph can be very effective as is shown in this writing by one GCSE student:

> As dawn breaks over this deserted, silent cove, lone rocks grow out of the water as the tide retreats. The beach is almost undisturbed, almost lonely without the screaming playful children. There is a longing for life as the golden sun creeps over the top of the cliffs. The grassy meadow at the peak is illuminated with a splash of light. As the morning grows, the shadows shorten. The shady cliffs begin to brighten as the waves lap at the sand. The crooked shadows of the rocks fade away and the sand grows golden from the light of the sun.
>
> A solitary figure shifts uneasily across the early morning shadow.
>
> Still all is quiet, but for the sound of water as it crashes gently onto the rocks. The day is warming and the sea rocks against the beach leaving patterns in the sand and uncovering hidden secrets as the tide washes away. The beach is clean and smooth, scarred only by that single set of footprints.

- In this example, the single sentence paragraph emphasises the isolation of the figure on the beach. It makes the reader pause and wonder who this figure is. The paragraph before hints at what is to come, with the reference to the beach being *almost undisturbed*, and the subsequent paragraph continues the idea with reference to the *single set of footprints*.

Test yourself

Write three paragraphs, one of which is a single sentence. Aim to create links between the paragraphs as shown in the example above. Remember the single sentence paragraph should be designed to have maximum impact on your reader. You could write your paragraphs on one of the following subjects.

(a) The First Exam

(b) The Job Interview

(c) The City at Night

Remember, your examiner will be assessing the ways you link paragraphs and the ways you use them for effect. Once you have written your three paragraphs, ask a friend or parent to comment on how well they work together.

19 Writing for audience

Know the facts

- The audience of a piece of writing is the intended reader, the person (or people) you are writing for. The way you write something is likely to be influenced by your intended audience.

Look at the following extracts. Which extract is intended for:

(a) an audience of primary school children?

(b) a teenage audience?

(c) an adult audience?

> **1** He wasn't your usual soap hunk. In fact, if the scruffy indie kid mooched past you in the street, you probably wouldn't give him a second look.
>
> *Bliss* March 2000
>
> **2** The government is planning an increase of up to 50% in adoptions to reduce the number of children living under local authority care, health ministers announced yesterday.
>
> *The Guardian* 8 July 2000
>
> **3** Sam came home early. His mother said 'Hello, Sam', Sam said hello to his mother. He walked into the garden and under the great tree. He stood quietly. He waited for his new friend to appear.

- The following features will have helped you to identify the intended audience:
  - the variety of sentence structures
  - the difficulty of the vocabulary
  - the subject matter
  - the use of formal or informal language.

- It is important that you take your intended reader into account whenever you plan and write something.

- Remember, in an exam you always have another unnamed audience – your examiner!

Test yourself

Write three short introductions to a holiday resort. Each introduction has a different audience. They are:

(a) children aged 7 to 10

(b) teenagers aged 16 to 17

(c) parents with young families.

You are writing about the same holiday resort each time, but you should aim to write about it in different ways to suit your different audiences. Think about:
  - the different features of the resort
  - the words you use
  - the complexity of the sentence structures you use.

Once you have written your introductions check that you can identify the audience of each by the way it has been written.

18

19

Know the facts

There are three different stances that the writer can adopt. S/he can write in:

- **the first person (I, we)**, which is often used for personal accounts, for example:

> At around this time **I** began walking backwards. **I** would arch **my** back and, placing **my** hands by my feet, **I** would scuttle like some demented crab about the house. **I** did this for about a year. **I** did it at home mainly, but **I** did it in public too, occasionally even going up and down the stairs of the bus this way. **I** probably did it to get noticed, but mainly **I** did it to irritate people.
>
> *Is That It?* by Bob Geldof

- **the second person (you)**, sometimes used to draw the reader into the text, for example:

> **Your** front door opens out on to some of the most empty and dangerous countryside in Britain. Hundreds of square miles of saturated earth and rotting peat, a kind of spongy version of the sea. When **you** were a kid **you** walked across the moors looking for dead bodies, but found tractor tyres instead, or fridge-freezers, or crash helmets, miles from anything or anywhere.
>
> *All Points North* by Simon Armitage

- **the third person (he, she, it, they)**, sometimes used to create a distance between the writer and the subject, for example:

> It was not until **she** reached Standard 1 that **her** troubles really began. Arithmetic was the subject by which the pupils were placed, and as **Laura** could not grasp the simplest rule with such small help as the mistress had time to give, **she** did not even know how to begin working out the sums and was permanently at the bottom of the class.
>
> *Lark Rise to Candleford* by Flora Thompson

- Aim to be familiar with the three different stances that you can use, and to experiment with them.

Test yourself

Choose an incident from your own childhood. Give an account of the same incident in the:

(a) first person (I, we)

(b) second person (you)

(c) third person (he, she, it, they).

Aim to write three or four sentences for each account.

Know the facts

Writers often try to influence the way their readers will react to the information they are presenting. In order to do this they use words or phrases that target particular emotions, words or phrases that make the readers feel something. Look at A to C:

A Politicians argue while thousands die in lonely agony.

B ... this shameful, shabby treatment of our war heroes.

C The streets are not safe whilst this evil monster is free to roam.

- Example A aims to make the reader feel pity by using the words *lonely agony*.

- Example B tries to appeal to a sense of national pride by referring to our *war heroes*. The words *shameful* and *shabby* are intended to make the reader feel that this is not right.

- Example C targets the reader's sense of fear and insecurity through the words *not safe*. The words *evil monster* emphasise this sense of danger.

- This is known as **emotive** use of language. It is a powerful tool to develop in your own writing.

Test yourself

Write the text for an advertisement appealing for help for abused animals. Use language emotively to make people feel disturbed and upset by what you tell them so that they will give money to help. Write about fifty words. You may want to use some of these words and phrases:

appalling conditions

permanently scarred

irreversible damage

shocking state

helpless

whining pitifully

bruised and battered

vulnerable

Know the facts

Generally, we adapt the way we speak according to our audience. Students tend not to speak to their teachers in the same ways as they speak to their friends.

(a) The language of the playground tends to be very informal:

(b) The language of the classroom tends to be more formal:

The same rules apply with writing. When writing a letter or an e-mail to a friend you would probably write **informally**. You would use the same kind of words that you would use if you were speaking, for example:

Hi Jaz,

How's things? Not much going on here at the mo tho it looks like things are gonna heat up ...

- Informal writing tends to contain slang and shortened words.

- When writing a letter to somebody you don't know or for business purposes, you would almost certainly use a more **formal** form of language, for example:

Dear Mr Jones,

Thank you for your invitation to attend for interview on 20 January at 9pm. I intend to travel the night before and would be delighted to stay with you ...

- Formal language does not contain slang and words are written in full.

Test yourself

1 Write two messages:

(a) To inform a friend that you will meet her after school, giving the time and the place. Use language informally.

(b) To explain to a teacher why you cannot attend detention that evening. Use language formally.

23 Setting

Know the facts

Writers of fiction create an environment in which their story takes place. This is the **setting**.

- It includes the place itself, the social and political background to the story, the weather, the time period in which it is set and the environmental factors which help to create the tone and atmosphere of the story.

This passage is from the opening of a short story. As you read it focus on what you learn about the setting.

> The time when the rains didn't come for three months and the sun was a yellow furnace in the sky was known as the Great Drought in Trinidad. It happened when everyone was expecting the sky to burst open with rain to fill the dry streams and water the parched earth.
>
> But each day was the same; the sun rose early in a blue sky, and all day long the farmers lifted their eyes, wondering what had happened to Parjanya, the rain god. They rested on their hoes and forks and wrung perspiration from their clothes, seeing no hope in labour, terrified by the thought that if no rain fell soon they would lose their crops and livestock and face starvation and death.
>
> In the tiny village of Las Lomas, out in his vegetable garden, Manko licked dry lips and passed a wet sleeve over his dripping face. Somewhere in the field a cow mooed mournfully, sniffing around for a bit of green in the cracked earth. The field was a desolation of drought. The trees were naked and barks peeled off trunks as if they were diseased. When the wind blew, it was heavy and unrelieving, as if the heat had taken all the spirit out of it.
>
> *A Drink of Water* by Sam Selvon

Test yourself

1 Make a list of all the different things you learn about the setting from the three paragraphs above.

2 Write your own opening to a short story. Focus on writing two or three paragraphs to create a clear setting in which the story can take place.

24 Characterisation

Know the facts

Most works of fiction revolve around a number of central characters. Writers reveal their characters to their readers in a variety of ways:

- Their appearance:

> He was a big man, grown brown and burnt from years of working on the land. His arms were bent and he had a crouching position even when he stood upright. When he laughed he showed more tobacco stain than teeth.

- Their words:

> 'The water belong to Rampersad,' Manko said. 'Is his own, and if he choose to sell it, is his business. We can't just go and take, that would be thiefing. You must never thief from another man, Sunny. That is a big, big sin. No matter what happen.'

- Their actions:

> The dog sprang up at the sound and moved with uncanny swiftness. Before Sunny could turn, it had sprung across the well, straight at the boy's throat.
>
> Manko scrambled over the fence, ripping away his clothes and drawing blood. He ran and cleared the well in a great jump, and tried to tear the beast away from the struggling boy. The dog turned, growling low in the throat as it faced this new attacker.
>
> *A Drink of Water* by Sam Selvon

What do you learn about Manko from each of these?

Test yourself

1 Create your own character. Decide what s/he looks like. Has s/he any distinguishing features such as a *crouching position* or *tobacco stained teeth*?

2 What kind of person is your character? What kinds of things would s/he say? How would s/he say them? What would they show about your character's beliefs?

3 How would your character react in a stressful or dangerous situation? Create a specific situation and show how s/he reacts.

Know the facts

When writing imaginatively, either in coursework or your exam, it is important to structure your story in an original and effective way. There are many different ways of structuring a story. Here are just a few of them:

The linear method: This follows the order of events as they happpen – the writer starts at the beginning and ends at the end. This is the most commonly used method.

Flashbacks: The ending of the story is placed at the beginning. Then the writer describes the events leading up to this by a series of memories or flashbacks. This allows the story to move easily between the past and the present. It is a useful device for dealing with things that have happened a long time ago.

The twist in the tale: The ending of the story is entirely unexpected, though when the reader looks back s/he can see that there were some clues. This helps to maintain the reader's interest right to the end. It is a technique often used successfully in ghost and mystery stories.

Test yourself

Choose one of the methods outlined above. Plan the outline for a piece of imaginative writing based on the title 'The Last Chance'. Your outline should clearly demonstrate how the chosen structure would work. Your aim is to interest and entertain your reader.

---

26 More about structure

Know the facts

Your examiner will be marking many responses to the same question. If you want to make a favourable impression you need to give careful thought to how you structure your ideas. The more you experiment with alternative structures now, the easier it will be to produce something different in your exam.

Here are some more ways of giving structure to stories:

Dual narrator: Two different characters are used to tell a story from contrasting viewpoints. These could be, for example, a boyfriend and girlfriend, a parent and child, a bully and victim, a footballer and manager. This allows the writer to explore different ideas and attitudes and is an interesting way of showing conflict.

The recurring idea or symbol: A single idea or symbol is used throughout the story. This could be the approach of a storm, a flower gradually losing its petals, a candle slowly burning, a developing nightmare or something similar. It helps to tie the parts of the story together. It can also be used to help create a sinister and threatening atmosphere.

The diary form: This enables the reader to get a very clear picture of the main character, the diary writer. His or her thoughts and feelings are revealed in relation to the things that have been happening, as recorded in the diary. It allows the writer to adopt an informal style and can be used to create humour.

Test yourself

Write diary entries for the following characters:

(a) A teenage boy or girl who has just been stood up on a date.

(b) A scientist who believes he is about to make a major breakthrough in his research.

(c) A prisoner during his first week in jail.

Aim to:

• capture the voice of the character

• make the situation convincing.

27 Writing to inform

Know the facts

- When you are writing to inform, your aim is to tell your reader about something or somebody. Informative writing in an encyclopedia is generally based on known facts:

> **school** (education) A place where learning can take place, usually classified according to whether it is for primary or secondary age pupils. Schools and schoolmasters were noted by Arabs to be in every Chinese town by 851; and primary and secondary schools were established in all 1000 sub-prefectures of China by 1107. The term can also denote a grouping of subjects, such as a 'humanities school'.
>
> *The Cambridge Encyclopedia* edited by David Crystal

- Often, however, informative writing also includes opinions:

> Let me tell you about a typical school day. First lesson, French, starts at approximately 8.50, after a ten-minute registration period with the grumpiest Form Tutor in the Universe. Then it's on to an hour of unrelenting boredom with Physics, followed by a brief but usually chat-packed break with the gang before facing the demanding challenge of surviving an hour on the tennis courts.

- To make informative writing interesting to read it is important to:
  - give an appropriate amount of detail
  - make your information relevant to your audience
  - vary the range of information you include.

Test yourself

A future employer has asked you to write a brief and informative account of yourself. Make a list of the appropriate points you want to include. Remember your account is likely to mix:

(a) facts about your education and any work experience you may have had

(b) your opinions about your attitudes to work and the kind of person you are – you might want to include things other people have said about you.

28 Writing to explain

Know the facts

- When you are writing to explain, your aim is to make something clear to your reader.

- Explanation often addresses the questions *What?, Why?, How?* When you explain you give answers.

A simple task might be to explain how to make a particular meal. Features of a good explanation would include:

- a clear outline of *what* ingredients are needed

- set of instructions which explains *how* to make it

- clear linking between the stages of the meal preparation.

- In an English exam you could be asked to draw on personal experience and explain a particular attitude or feeling, as in the following exam task.

> Choose an event from your past that has particular significance for you.
>
> Explain what happened and your feelings about it.

- When you explain you give answers. What questions might you need to ask yourself in the task above?

- Writing to explain is tightly structured with ideas closely linked together. Here are some phrases often used in Writing to explain:

Because of this ...	This was due to ...
Inevitably ...	Subsequently ...
As a result of ...	Finally ...

Test yourself

Read the exam task again. Follow these stages:

- Ask yourself a series of questions: What event? What happened? How? Why? What did I feel at the time? What consequences did it have? Why were these significant? How do I feel about it now? What difference has it made to me?

- Decide the order in which you would deal with the answers to these questions.

29 Writing to describe

Know the facts

- When writing to describe, you are trying to paint a picture with words. Your aim is to give your reader as clear a picture as you can of the person, place or event that you are describing.

The following paragraph, in which the writer describes a room and its inhabitant, is the opening of a well-known short story. Read it carefully.

> Imagine if you can, a small room, hexagonal in shape, like the cell of a bee. It is lighted neither by window nor by lamp, yet it is filled with a soft radiance. There are no apertures for ventilation, yet the air is fresh. There are no musical instruments, and yet, at the moment that my meditation opens, this room is throbbing with melodious sounds. An armchair is in the centre, by its side a reading-desk – that is all the furniture. And in the armchair there sits a swaddled lump of flesh – a woman, about five feet high, with a face as white as a fungus. It is to her that the little room belongs.
>
> *The Machine Stops* by E.M. Forster

In this paragraph the writer uses:

- adjectives   a soft radiance
  the air is fresh
  melodious sounds
- similes   like the cell of a bee
  a face as white as a fungus
- metaphor   a swaddled lump of flesh.

These are all features of descriptive writing.

Test yourself

Write a paragraph in which you describe a person sitting in a room. Use a range of appropriate adjectives. Aim to include two similes and one metaphor. Have a clear picture of the person and the room in your mind before you start to write. You could start *Imagine, if you can, ...*

30 Writing to persuade

Know the facts

- When you are writing to persuade, your aim is to make your reader do something or believe something.

Writing to persuade is commonly found in:

- adverts, where the writer is trying to persuade you to buy a particular product
- charity appeals, where the writer is trying to persuade you to give your support.

Some common features of writing to persuade are:

- **rhetorical questions** that are designed to make the reader think, for example:

  Is a third pint worth a life?

- **exaggeration** where words are used to make something seem greater than it is, for example:

  The world's best carpet sale – ever!

- **repetition** of words or phrases for emphasis, for example:

  Millions of people will contract AIDS this year; millions of people will die of AIDS this year.

- **group of three** where ideas are linked together in groups of three to create maximum impact, for example:

  For a truly carefree holiday where the sun always shines, the faces are always smiling and the nightlife sizzles, come to Barbados.

- **emotive language** where words are used to influence the reader's feelings directly, for example:

  It is the weakest and most vulnerable babies who are the first to be ruthlessly abandoned.

Aim to use some of these features when you write to persuade.

Test yourself

Write the text for an e-mail message to a friend. Your aim is to persuade him or her to come and help you over the weekend as you and your family are moving house. You know it won't be much fun, but you really want him or her to be there. Aim to use at least three of the features of persuasive writing listed above.

Know the facts

- When writing to argue, your aim is to present and develop a particular point of view. Look at the following.

> **Match Of The Day – Should BBC have saved it?**
>
> **YES**
>
> What a blow for soccer fans. The BBC has lost the right to show Premiership football highlights on Saturday night, so that is the end of Match Of The Day. The Beeb offered the soccer authorities £41m a year, £20m less than ITV.
>
> When Greg Dyke took over as boss of the BBC, he promised that sport would be a priority, and what happens? One of the most popular programmes on telly is lost to ITV. There is already no live Premiership soccer on terrestrial telly. What do we pay our licence fees for? Fans don't want adverts in soccer shows. The BBC should have pulled out all the stops to save Match Of The Day.
>
> **NO**
>
> The BBC just can't win, can they? On the one hand they are criticised from all quarters for wasting licence payers' money and whenever the licence fee goes up, but on the other hand they are lambasted for not splashing out loads of our money on football!
>
> The BBC were quite right not to hand over even more cash – our money – to the soccer chiefs. Goodness knows, football clubs and players are rich enough already, and does it really matter which channel soccer is shown on? Fans can still watch the games if they want, and the BBC can put the money they have saved towards producing more worthwhile shows.
>
> *Manchester Evening News* 15 June 2000

Notice how there is a mixture here of opinion:

> The BBC were quite right not to hand over even more cash – our money – to the soccer chiefs.

and fact:

> There is already no live Premiership soccer on terrestrial telly.

Notice some of the features of language:

- rhetorical question   What do we pay our licence fees for?

- exclamation   ... for not splashing out loads of our money on football!

- emotive language   What a blow for soccer fans.

Test yourself

Your local newspaper runs a weekly 'point of view' section. Write a letter to the paper expressing your point of view on a local issue. It could be:

(a) the lack of local facilities for young people

(b) a proposal to build a new shopping centre on land currently used as playing fields

(c) the need for more cycle paths

(d) the decision to close a local school

(e) something else ... .

Aim to use:

- both fact and opinion
- a range of language features for effect.

Know the facts

Extending the argument

Written arguments can be based simply on personal experience and opinion. Sometimes, however, you may not have a clear-cut point of view on a particular situation or topic. You might find that you have some sympathy with both sides of the argument. If that is the case you can use points from both sides of the argument to develop a wider discussion.

Developing key points

When writing a developed argument it is essential that you plan the key points. These are the main points you want to make in the course of your argument. They can be taken from either side of the argument.

Using counter-argument

- Counter-argument is often used when people put forward an argument. It means admitting that your opponents have a point, then saying something to 'counter' or to go against it, for example:

  It is often claimed that caning would put an end to bad behaviour in schools but, in reality, when caning was allowed there was still a great deal of bad behaviour and exam results were not as good as they are today.

- The word *but* is often used when the writer is using counter-argument.

Helpful words and phrases

- When discussing a range of different points of view it is often helpful to link ideas by using some of the following words or phrases.

  Alternatively ...

  On the other hand ...

  Some people believe that ...

  In contrast to this ...

  Nevertheless ...

  Similarly ...

  Perhaps the most important point is ...

  This suggests that ...

Test yourself

Some people argue that there is inadequate sex education in secondary schools. Argue your point of view on this subject. Follow these stages:

1 Work out what you think about this.

2 List a number of points for and against increasing the amount of sex education in secondary schools.

3 Plan what points you want to make. These are the key points of your argument. Aim to include a range of facts and opinions. These could be based on national statistics and/or on personal experience. (Remember, in an English exam you can always invent statistics.)

4 Decide on the best order for the key points to ensure they have maximum impact.

33 Writing to advise

Know the facts

- We live in a society which is constantly being given advice – advice on diet, exercise, finances, what to wear, which films to watch, how to find a boyfriend or girlfriend and so on.

- Writing to advise often has particular features that you could imitate in your own writing. Read the following extract and the annotations carefully.

Changing (your) workout can be a key factor to improving your fitness level. If (you) run on the treadmill regularly but never row, use the rowing machine and you (could) raise your heart rate more than on a machine that your body is accustomed to using. (Alternatively,) if you're stuck in a thrice-weekly gym routine *why not try something in the open air?* A game of tennis *should get* your heart and lungs working overtime and it's fun too. Remember to always (wear) your trainers when exercising out-of-doors (and *don't forget*) your warm-up and cool-down routines.

addresses the reader directly

uses the conditional tense

gives you options

uses rhetorical questions

uses imperatives

Test yourself

You are asked by your Form Tutor to write an advice sheet for incoming Year 7 pupils on how to survive life in your school. Write the opening 150 words of your advice sheet. Aim to include all of the features associated with writing to advise.

34 Writing to analyse

Know the facts

- Writing to analyse is used when writing about a poem or a scientific experiment, or when writing about why a particular team won or lost a football match.

- When you analyse something you examine it closely. Writing to analyse involves explanation of how and why things happen.

- The language of analysis is usually:
  - very precise
  - not dependent on personal feelings
  - formal and impersonal
  - heavily reliant on technical terms
  - associated with facts and figures.

Test yourself

Read the following extract. Identify in it as many of the above features as you can.

London, which led the country into a boom, is now leading the way out with a 2.4% fall in house prices over the past three months. The average price in the capital has fallen by more than £1000 per month from £148 672 at the end of March to £145 104 at the end of June.

Nationally, house prices were unchanged in the second quarter of the year, the first time that prices have not risen since the third quarter of 1995. But the sharp rises earlier this year mean that the average house price, £84 422, is still 11.3% ahead of a year ago.

Four successive interest rate rises and the abolition of mortgage tax relief have caused the market to grind to a halt, according to Halifax.

The Guardian 8 July 2000

33

34

35

Know the facts

- When you review something you assess it. In English you might be asked to write a review of a book or a play or a film.

- A review is usually written in the present tense.

- A review usually involves:
  - a brief summary of at least part of the plot
  - hints at parts of the plot not included in the summary
  - relevant comments on the subject
  - a summative assessment or recommendation.

Read the following review of a film:

A Life Less Ordinary

Stars: Ewan McGregor and Cameron Diaz

A brief summary ——— **Plot:** Down-on-his-luck janitor Ewan McGreogr loses his job and his girlfriend, so decides to take revenge on his nasty boss, holding him up at gunpoint and kidnapping his beautiful but spoilt daughter (Cameron Diaz). Our Ewan turns out to be a rather inept hoodlum but, fortunately,

Hints at what else happens ——— the streetwise Diaz seems to have more of an idea of how to pull the abduction stunt off. In the meantime, a couple of angels (the divine Holly Hunter and Delroy Lindo) are sent down to ensure that the mismatched couple fall in love ... This doesn't always

Comment ——— come off, but some great scenes – a botched heist, McGregor's pathetic attempts to deliver a ransom demand and a fantasy karaoke number in a bar – plus the glamour and charisma of the two stars make this an enjoyable

Recommendation ——— feelgood ride. Also stars Ian Holm and Stanley Tucci.

TV Quick 23–29 September, Issue 39

Test yourself

Write a review of a film you have watched or a book you have read recently. It is to be included in a magazine for readers your age. Your review should be no more than 120 words. Before writing decide:

(a) the key points you are going to include in the summary

(b) the hints you are going to give

(c) the comments you are going to make

(d) the recommendation you are going to give.

It may help you to model your review on the example given.

33

34

35

Know the facts

- When you comment on something you are giving your opinion on it. 'I don't like this poem' is an opinion or a simple comment. In your English writing, however, you are being asked to do more than simply give opinions when you write to comment.

- Your examiner is looking for your ability to:
  - justify your opinions
  - refer to the text to support your opinions
  - link your ideas logically
  - develop your comments intelligently.

Here are the first lines of a poem called 'Valentine':

> Not a red rose or a satin heart.
> I give you an onion.
> It is a moon wrapped in brown paper.
> It promises light
> Like the careful undressing of love.
>
> by Carol Ann Duffy

You could comment on these lines in these ways:

- Simple comment

  It is good the way she gives her lover an onion rather than a proper valentine.

- Comment supported by reference to the text

  In these lines the writer chooses to give an unusual valentine present. She rejects the more conventional presents of 'a red rose or a satin heart' and compares the onion to 'a moon wrapped in brown paper'.

- In an exam you should aim to support and develop your comments.

  In these lines the writer chooses to give an unusual valentine present. She rejects the more conventional presents of 'a red rose or a satin heart' and compares the onion to 'a moon wrapped in brown paper'. This suggests it contains something special that is hidden away from sight. It 'promises light', which makes it seem desirable, and this is echoed in the comparison to the 'careful undressing of love' which carries with it sexual connotations.

Test yourself

Read the next stanza of this poem:

> Here.
> It will blind you with tears
> Like a lover.
> It will make your reflection
> A wobbling photo of grief.

Write your comments on these lines. Aim to:

(a) develop your comments

(b) support your comments by referring to the text.

37   Setting out leaflets, advice sheets and newsletters

Know the facts

- In every area of modern life we are surrounded by information in the form of leaflets, advice sheets and newsletters.

- Their main purpose is to give information in a quick, clear and interesting way.

- Some typical features of these are:
  - headings
  - subheadings
  - bullet points
  - use of different size and types of fonts
  - underlining and bold print
  - illustrations, graphs and diagrams.

- Writers of these kinds of materials often use slogans and puns to help put their message across.

- A **slogan** is a distinctive phrase, associated with a particular company or charity.

- A **pun** occurs where there is a play on words.

- Producing a leaflet requires skills in design as well as in writing. However, if you are asked to produce one in an examination it is the organisation and content of the text that is important. Your examiner is assessing you on your writing skills, not on your design skills. You would not normally be expected to do pictures or to spend time on fancy headings or trying to write in columns.

Test yourself

Write the text for a leaflet to be used in a careers lesson. It could contain general advice about interview techniques or relate to a specific area of work. Aim to use:

(a) a heading and subheadings

(b) underlining for emphasis

(c) bullet points

(d) a slogan and a pun.

These all help to demonstrate your awareness of the particular form.

38   Writing reports

Know the facts

There are several different kinds of reports. Students at school often receive an annual report on their work and progress. A housebuyer might commission a report on the condition of a particular property. The most common kind of report, however, is the newspaper report.

A newspaper report tells the story of something that has happened. Journalists inform their readers of recent local, national and international events.

Newspaper reports tend to follow a pattern. The first paragraph usually contains the main points of the story and aims to grab the reader's attention. People tend to read newspapers quickly and often decide whether to continue reading on the basis of the first paragraph. Frequently, the first paragraph answers the questions: Who? What? Where? When? Why? How? The following paragraphs then develop these points, providing further information.

Test yourself

Which of these questions are answered in this opening paragraph from a newspaper report: Who? What? Where? When? Why? How? What are the answers to each of these questions?

> Fifa, world football's governing body, appeared in confusion yesterday over a death threat allegedly made against one of its executive members during the contest to host the 2006 World Cup.
>
> *The Guardian* 8 July 2000

39 Features of reports

Know the facts

As seen in the last Unit, one typical feature of a newspaper report is an opening paragraph which summarises the main points of the story. Other typical features of reports include:

- An interesting headline which draws attention to the report.

  This might be:

  a rhetorical question – Is this justice?

  an exclamation – Our last chance!

  a pun – Bird's flight for freedom

- Writing in the past tense, as the relevant events have already happened:

  A scuffle broke out when police arrested a youth in connection with the incident.

- Brief descriptions of the main people involved in the story:

  His mother, Kate, 44, a leading member of the Golf Club Association, refused to comment.

- Quotations from people connected with the story:

  Mark McAvoy, who observed the attack from a safe distance, said, 'Nobody could have stopped him. He was like a mad man.'

39 40 41 42

Test yourself

Write a report for a local newspaper on:

Local school raises £10 000 for children's charity.

Before starting to write your report:

- invent names, dates and other relevant details.

- invent quotations from relevant people, for example Mayor, teacher, charity manager, pupil

- decide the order in which you will deal with the details

- work out the wording of your opening paragraph and decide on a headline.

40 Writing articles

Know the facts

- Articles appear in magazines, too. They can cover an enormous range of subjects from 'Your Computer Hard Drive' to 'Love in the 21st Century'.

- They often combine a range of different types of writing including writing to advise, to inform, to describe, to argue and to persuade, as is shown in the extract below. As you read the article try to identify the purpose and audience, the tone and the tense in which it is written.

> Look around your house. Is there a child slumped heavily in a sofa or armchair? Look closely at that child. Are her cheeks chubby? Does her tummy gently flop over the too-tight size14 jeans?
>
> Concern is growing over the vast number of overweight children currently spending far too much of their time in those sofas and armchairs. This is the generation which has been raised on chocolate breakfast cereals, high-fat snacks and convenience meals. This is the generation transported to school by car, allowed to miss P.E. for the flimsiest of excuses, cosseted by guilt-ridden, overworked, overstressed, 'yes you can have a television and video and computer and Playstation and anything else you like in your bedroom as long as we don't have to talk about it' parents. This is the generation which, as we gaze fondly at them reaching for another bag of high-fat, high-calorie crisps, is doomed to die prematurely.

Common features of articles are:

- they target purpose and audience closely
- they are less formal than reports
- they have a distinctive style and tone
- they are written in the present tense.

Test yourself

Choose one of the following subjects.

(a) Sport in schools

(b) Friendships on the Internet

(c) Weight worries among teenagers

Decide on your purpose and your audience. Write the opening two paragraphs for an article on your subject.

41 Setting out a letter

Know the facts

This shows the normal layout for a formal letter.

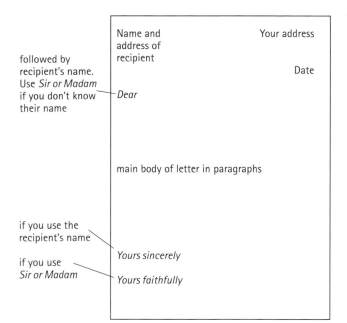

followed by recipient's name. Use *Sir or Madam* if you don't know their name

Name and address of recipient

Your address

Date

Dear

main body of letter in paragraphs

if you use the recipient's name

if you use *Sir or Madam*

Yours sincerely

Yours faithfully

- In an informal letter you still need to include your address and the date but not the name and address of the person to whom you are writing. Address the recipient by his or her first name or the name by which you usually call them. An informal ending is usually *Love from, Best wishes, See you soon* or something similar, followed by your signature.

Test yourself

Read the following, then set out two letters in reply, using the correct form each time. There is no need to write the whole letter. Concentrate on getting the layout right.

(a) Fast Foods has a Saturday vacancy for a young person, aged between 16 and 18 years. Apply in writing to Ms K. Keenan, Manageress, Fast Foods, 126 Shipley Rd., Cantown, CA5 6OW.

(b) You are invited to Jayne and Paul's engagement party.

21st July. 8 'til late.

Bring a bottle.

Hope to see you.

42 Content of letters

Know the facts

In an exam you may be asked to write a letter for a particular purpose and audience. For example, your purpose might be to persuade or to inform or to argue, your audience might be a friend, the readers of a local or national newspaper or a figure of authority such as a councillor or Member of Parliament.

Once you have worked out the purpose and audience of your letter there are certain points to remember while you are writing.

- Start with a clear opening statement which identifies the issue.
- Write in the first person using either *I* or *we*.
- Write in the present tense.
- Organise your ideas into a logical order.
- Use paragraphs to reflect that logical order.
- Develop your ideas appropriately using examples.
- Mix factual detail and opinion.
- Use rhetorical questions for effect.
- Use emotive language for effect.
- Emphasise your main points in your concluding paragraph.

Test yourself

Write a letter to your local Member of Parliament in which you argue for better sports provision in schools. Work out:

(a) purpose   (b) audience.

Here are some ideas to help you start:

— the importance of having healthy children
— variety of sports provision leads to more interest
— many schools have no access to a swimming pool
— sports halls could be kept open out of school hours
— some schools are selling off their playing fields to make money.

Remember to:

— set out your letter correctly
— include some or all of the features listed above.

43 Thinking about the question

Know the facts 🔖

- The first ten minutes of any writing task are probably the most important. It is in these ten minutes that you choose what you are going to write and how you are going to write it.

- First you need to pick your task carefully. In making your choice you must be sure that:
  - you understand the task
  - you have plenty to write about.

- It is important to break the task down into sections when you first read it, by asking yourself some questions. Look at this example task:

  Write an article for a magazine aimed at either young men or young women, in which you argue that smoking should:

  either be banned in public places

  or be allowed in public places.

You might ask yourself the following questions to break the task down.

> Q1 What do I have to write?
>
> A A magazine article.
>
> Q2 What is my purpose (the reason for writing)?
>
> A To argue **either** to ban **or** allow smoking in public places.
>
> Q3 Who is my audience (the people intended to read it)?
>
> A Young men **or** young women and the examiner.
>
> Q4 What kind of writing is it?
>
> A Writing to argue.

Test yourself 🔖

Apply the four questions above to this writing task.

As a victim of a recent mugging, write a letter to a local newspaper arguing that punishment today is not harsh enough.

44 Openings

Know the facts 🔖

A recent Principal Examiners' Report states:

> The time given to planning was a significant factor in the candidates' performance in writing. The paper makes it clear that candidates should spend about ten minutes planning and sequencing their ideas before writing. Examiners noted a clear link between the degree of careful planning and the quality of response. Without question, time spent on thinking and planning does greatly improve candidates' writing and results in the award of a higher mark.

Students know they should plan, their teachers frequently remind them to plan and the examiners report that writing is much better when it has been planned. So what goes wrong?

Basically people panic. They think they haven't enough time. Besides, the plan is not going to gain them any marks. What they forget is that the plan is the route to organised writing and, consequently, to higher marks.

- After you have thought about the exam question, one of the first stages of planning is to brainstorm ideas. You can do this by asking yourself a series of questions: How? What? Where? When? Why? Who?

Test yourself 🔖

As part of the way your school/college tries to help new students to settle in, it has asked you to write a lively and entertaining 'Welcome to ...' leaflet which will give advice and information from a student's point of view. Your leaflet should give:

(a) information about the school/college

(b) practical tips about what to expect

(c) guidance on how to survive the first few weeks.

Use the brainstorm model below to gather ideas.

45 Further strategies for planning

Know the facts

It is not enough to simply gather a range of ideas. Once again the Examiners' Report states that:

Too many candidates started to write without a clear sense of direction, which could have been achieved with more time spent thinking at the start. Similarly many candidates wrote at great length, sometimes five to six sides, when the same skills, and more, could have been better demonstrated in two to three sides.

- You wouldn't start a journey without a plan of how to get to your destination and it is the same with your writing. You need to know where you are going and how you are going to get there.

To achieve this you need to plan the order in which you are going to deal with your ideas. You could do this by simply numbering the different ideas you had in your brainstorm. At this stage you need to decide what to keep in and what to miss out. A brief paragraph plan, outlining what each paragraph will contain, is also a useful way of organising ideas and planning the shape your writing will take.

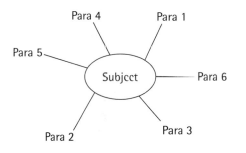

Test yourself

Look back at your brainstorm from Unit 44.

(a) Think about how you could group or connect your different ideas. (You could link them with arrows.)

(b) Think about the order in which you will write about your ideas. (It may help to number them.)

(c) Make a brief plan, outlining the content of each paragraph. Remember this is a plan. You do not need to write in sentences.

46 Openings

Know the facts

The opening of any piece of writing is very important. It is your best opportunity to:

- capture your reader's attention

- make a favourable first impression.

The following first sentence was written in response to the exam task 'Describe your ideal home'.

> In my ideal home I would have lots of different rooms all in different colours.

- This is a very plain opening. It doesn't really make the reader want to read on.

Now read these more imaginative openings:

> Walk up my cobbled drive. See the distant castle turrets. Smell the fragrant scent of jasmine.

- By using the imperatives, *walk*, *see* and *smell* in quick succession, and by appealing to the different senses, the writer has drawn the reader into the scene.

> As the curtains are drawn to one side, the light sweeps through the darkened rooms like a shimmering sword.

- The use of a simile helps to emphasise the movement from dark to light in an interesting way.

> Have you ever seen a place of such beauty you gasped with delight?

- The use of the rhetorical question invites the reader to find out more about this place of beauty.

43 44 45 46

Test yourself

Think of two different openings for each of the following writing tasks.

(a) Describe a city centre in the daytime.

(b) Write an article for a sports magazine about a sport you are interested in.

(c) Write a letter to a friend advising him/her on what to take on holiday.

Aim to use some of the techniques outlined above.

Know the facts

- Sometimes students don't take time to think about making their ending effective. This leaves the examiner with a negative impression.

- As you come to the end of a piece of writing it is important to consider how you are going to finish it. Here are various techniques you can try:

- **Leave the reader with a new idea:** at the end of writing an argument students often simply summarise the points they have already made. It can often be more effective to throw in a really strong point right at the end, for example:

> The arguments against fox hunting seem very strong until, that is, they are applied to fishing. The general public seems far less willing to defend the rights of the fish to swim freely in the rivers of this country than they are for the fox to have the freedom of the farmlands. But then fishing is a very popular sport!

- **Ask a question:** a question can make an effective ending to almost any piece of writing. Look at how it is used at the end of this writing about running:

> We can't all win the Olympics but we can all do something to improve our fitness levels. Running's my way. What's yours?

- **Use aposiopesis:** this creates the sense that there is more to follow or that the reader must work out the rest of the story. The following endings are taken from pieces of creative writing.

>   He walked slowly down the hill. He would be back ...
>   She spread out her arms and swam for the shore ...

Test yourself

Think of two different endings for the writing tasks below. You could match the endings to your openings from Unit 46. Use some of the techniques above.

(a) Describe a city centre in the daytime.

(b) Write an article for a sports magazine about a sport you are interested in.

(c) Write a letter to a friend advising him/her on what to take on holiday.

---

48 **Checking your work**

Know the facts

You should spend at least five minutes checking your work. Use this time to read what you have written – not what you *think* you have written – and to check that:

- it makes clear sense

- the punctuation is appropriate

- the word endings are correct

- your spelling is accurate.

Here, a student writes about her experience of being bullied. Notice the corrections she makes:

> *March. Up*
> It all started last ~~march up~~ until then I
> had lots of friends and I was generally
> happy. Yes I had problems but just ones I
> could sort out just like everybody ~~eles~~,   *else*
> but then things began to change. In march
> last year I could feel something was
> changing and my friends were ~~strange~~
> ~~distant~~ to me.
>   *strangely distant*
>
> *so-called*
> One morning I walked into school and none
> of my ~~so-called~~ friends were speaking to
> me. I spent the day feeling sad and lonely,
> trying to think what I had done wrong. I   *, when*
> ~~couldent~~ wait for the bell but ~~when it came~~   *it came*
> *couldn't* things only got ~~more worse~~. Tina and
> ~~sammy~~ were at the bus stop and they just   *worse*
> *Sammy* ignored me while my other friends started
> making sarcastic comments and laughing. I
> felt so upset I could ~~of cried instead~~ I   *have cried.*
> just turned away from them and ran and   *Instead*
> ran ~~untitl~~ I reached my front door.
> *until*

Test yourself

Correct the next paragraph of this extract:

When I got home I sat and cryed. I couldent work out what I had done that was suposed to be so bad I was shaking and had a bad headache so I whent to bed early. I didn't want my mum to know what had happened as it would upset her. Once I got to bed I stopped shaking and started to feel carmer though it was a long time befor I got to sleep.

Know the facts

Writers often redraft their material many times. In order to get it just right they change words, sentences and whole paragraphs. They take things out and add them in. You don't have time in an exam to completely redraft a piece of writing. You do have time to alter punctuation and vocabulary in order to improve the final product.

Read the following carefully. It shows how the extract from the previous Unit could be improved using simple redrafting techniques.

> a few close   Until
>
> It all started last March. ~~Up until~~ then I had ~~lots of~~ friends and I was generally happy. Yes, I had problems, but ~~just~~ ones
>
> .B I could sort out just like everybody else, ~~but~~ then things began to change. In March last year I could ~~feel~~ something was sense
>
> different ~~changing~~ and my friends were strangely distant to me.   becoming
>
> One morning I walked into school and none of my so-called friends were speaking to me. I spent the day feeling sad and lonely, trying to think what I had done wrong. I couldn't wait for the finally
>
> deteriorated bell but, when it ~~came~~, things only ~~got~~ arrived ~~worse~~. Tina and Sammy were at the bus stop and they just ignored me while my other friends started making sarcastic comments and laughing. I felt so upset I
>
> cruelly could have cried. Instead, I just turned away from them and ran and ran until I reached my front door.
>
>   the safety of

Test yourself

Redraft the next paragraph from the extract:

When I got home I sat and cried. I couldn't work out what I had done that was supposed to be so bad. I was shaking and had a bad headache so I went to bed early. I didn't want my mum to know what had happened as it would upset her. Once I got to bed I stopped shaking and started to feel calmer though it was a long time before I got to sleep.

Know the facts

- Arrive for your exam in good time and well prepared. Have a good pen and a spare.

- Read the questions carefully. Choose the one you can do best in the time available.

- Underline or highlight important words or phrases in the question.

- Identify purpose, audience and form.

- Plan your ideas carefully. You need to decide:
  - what you are going to say
  - the order in which you are going to say it
  - how you are going to say it.

- Remember, your plan is not marked but it will help you get better marks in your writing.

- Think about the form of your writing. If it's a letter, leaflet or article, you will need to include additional presentational features.

- Think about the tone of your writing. Should it be formal or informal?

- Aim to impress your reader by:
  - expressing your ideas clearly
  - using a range of sentence structures
  - using a range of vocabulary.

Aim for a high level of technical accuracy. Think about:
  - paragraphing
  - punctuation
  - tenses
  - spelling.

- Keep your eye on the clock. Make sure you bring your writing to a suitable conclusion even if it's not the one you had planned.

- Allow five minutes to check your work carefully.

Test yourself

Go through the above carefully. Make sure you understand each point.

47

48

49

50

Know the facts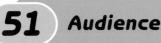

- It is vital to work out the intended **audience** and **purpose** of a piece of non-fiction text before you can work on the text further. Think about the following texts and their intended audience.

Text	Audience
the front page of a quality newspaper	somebody wanting the news in detail
the letters page of a teenage magazine	a teenager relaxing
a full page advert for a foreign holiday	a potential holiday-maker
a page in a dictionary	a student or somebody doing a crossword
a page in a geography textbook	a geography student

- Remember to think about audience when you are looking at a variety of different types of text on the same theme. For example, a journalist might decide to do a piece of writing about football, but they would still have to decide on the *audience* – would they be writing for the players themselves, the fans, the financial backers? The way the writer approached their writing would vary considerably depending on their decision.

Test yourself

1 Look at this list of texts, then decide who the *audience* is.

  (a) a flyer for a new local video rental outlet

  (b) the back of a branflakes box

  (c) the front page of a tabloid newspaper

2 As you see various texts during your day, think about who they are for – their *audience*.

Know the facts

- Once the audience has been established, a writer can begin to consider the purpose of a text – what the text is supposed to *do*. One of the main purposes of fiction texts is to entertain. However, non-fiction texts come in different forms and have different purposes:
  - A tourist leaflet is written to persuade people to visit a particular place.
  - League tables give information on the performance of teams.
  - History books explain historical facts.
  - A magazine article might argue a point of view.

- We can't necessarily call the examples above *factual* writing because although they are all about factual content, two actually contain the author's *opinion*: the tourist leaflet and the magazine article. (Read section 57, Bias, for more on this.)

- Once the writer has decided on the *aim* of their writing, they can make other decisions, such as what the content will be, what it will look like and what style of writing they will choose.

Test yourself

1 Decide what the *purpose* is of each of the texts that we looked at in section 51, Audience.

  (a) a flyer for a new local video rental outlet

  (b) the back of a branflakes box

  (c) the front page of a tabloid newspaper

2 Think about the various texts you've seen during the day, and work out what they have been written to do – their *purpose*.

51
52
53
54

Know the facts

- **Facts** are indisputable. They can be proved either by observation or by reference to a reliable written or visual source.

Fact one: The weight of a piece of steak bought at the local butcher's is 150 grams.

We can prove this by placing the meat on a set of scales and observing the reading on the dial. This gives us a *factual* statement on the weight of the steak.

Fact two: Henry the Eighth had six wives.

We can prove this is a *factual* statement by referring to standard history textbooks. We can look at three or four to be certain but they will all agree on the above *fact*.

- You can expect to find facts in writing wherever accuracy is essential. Car maintenance manuals would be one example where clear facts are needed to help the D.I.Y. mechanic maintain his/her own engine in safety. Sports reporting is another example; in a football report fans want to know the names of the scorers and the actual score. Also, of course, legal documents contain accurate information – a factual mistake could lead to a miscarriage of justice or an expensive financial settlement.

Test yourself

Which of the following are *factual* statements?

1 The chemical symbol for silver is Ag.

2 Tom Cruise starred in the film 'Mission Impossible'.

3 Pete Sampras is the finest tennis player there has ever been.

4 Cornwall is the English county with the most miles of coastline.

Know the facts

- An **opinion** is something which cannot be proved by methods such as observation or reference to reliable written or visual sources. It is your own idea on a subject; it may or may not be based on factual evidence but it is essentially your, or somebody's, *viewpoint*.

Opinion one: Bass is the best-tasting beer in the world.

This is an *opinion* statement since it is a personal viewpoint. There are literally thousands of beers in the world and there will be a huge variety of opinions as to which tastes the best. It can have little factual basis.

Opinion two: England are the worst side in Test cricket.

Although there is more of a factual base here it is still an *opinion* as the composition of teams and their form changes constantly.

- Feature articles in newspapers are often there to present *opinion* either as entertainment or as a starting point for serious debate. Novelists often use their novels to give an *opinion* on our world or human behaviour.

Test yourself

Which of the following are statements of *opinion*?

1 'Reservoir Dogs' is the most violent film ever made.

2 Manchester United were European Champions in club football in 1999.

3 Britain has the most successful education system in the world.

4 English education would be even better if we gave every child in the country a lap top computer for school work.

55 Distinguishing between fact and opinion

Know the facts

- Previous examples of **fact** and **opinion** have been quite clear cut and straightforward. However, on many occasions it is much more difficult to distinguish between the two. In many cases writers are quite happy for us to accept as fact what are essentially opinionated pieces of writing. How many times have you heard the remark, 'It must be true! It was in the paper!'?

- Newspaper articles, even in the quality broadsheets, are a mixture of fact and opinion. How would you judge this piece of writing?

> Once again our songwriters have proved to be miserable flops! Once again we have proved that we have lost the art of writing attractive pop songs! Our performance in the Eurovision Song Contest was abysmal. It has been a long time since a British entry triumphed.

- There is only one fact – the length of time since a British win. But the writer has used this to build up his/her own opinions. His/her opinions may or may not be valid – but they are opinions.

- Surveys are another source of confusion. Fifty-seven per cent of the country, for instance, might favour a certain chocolate bar, but they are a sample; maybe a well-selected sample, but statistics of this kind are not factual statements. They are a guide to certain attitudes at a certain time, but only a guide, not a fact.

Test yourself

Identify which sentences are fact and which are opinion in the following article.

> The latest opinion poll shows that 81% of the voting population sampled wish to become the 51st state of America. This shows how much the people wish to leave the Common Market. We are fed up being told what to do by Brussels. We feel more American than European! The survey was conducted in a sample of 27 voters at 2am on January 1 2000 outside The Westminster Arms in Central London.

56 Following an argument

Know the facts

- An **argument** is usually put together using a mixture of fact and opinion. The writer will use well-established facts on which to base and develop opinions. The argument may well present both sides of a case. The argument may draw a definite conclusion favouring one side or the other or it may leave it to the reader to decide. Remember, however, that any conclusion is an opinion.

Read the following article.

> Fox-hunting is a regular part of the country scene in England. Although many people see it as a violent sport, it is a popular English tradition. Many farmers belong to hunts and are happy to let hunters hunt on their land. People from all walks of life take part, often following the hunt on foot. There is no doubt that the fox can die a painful death inflicted by the dogs but if we let these emotions rule, many jobs would be lost in a hunting ban.

- The first step in following the argument is to list the points for and against, for example:

  For: it is a popular English tradition
              many jobs depend on it

  Against: the fox dies a cruel death

(Arguments *for* a ban are often a response based on emotions rather than facts.)

- Listing in full the points in an argument will help you to see the development of the argument, and the balance of points made between one side and another.

Test yourself

List fully the points made for and against compulsory team sport in schools in the following article.

> Sport is an essential part of growing up as a fit person. Pupils may be embarrassed by their body shape and their lack of skill but activity at a young age will save the country money on health care in years to come. It may be degrading to stand in lines while teams are picked, but being part of a winning team will compensate for that. The losers will learn a valuable lesson in accepting defeat with dignity.

Know the facts 🔊

- If you were playing in an inter-school football match, your parents or carers would be expected to support *your* team, rather than the team from the other school, because *you* are playing: in other words, they are **biased** in your favour. Similarly, the writer of the tourist leaflet mentioned in section 52, Purpose, might be biased in favour of the place they are promoting.

- Bias is stronger than opinion – a person's *opinions* may change, but their *bias* for or against something may not and is more deep-rooted. In a recent General Election campaign, the Leader of the Opposition said that if the Government was re-elected:

> I warn you that you will be cold, when fuel charges are used as a tax system that the rich don't notice and the poor can't afford; ... I warn you not to go into the streets alone after dark ...

He/she firmly believes what he/she is saying. There is no mention of the other party's point of view and the speaker doesn't give the other party a chance to put their case.

- It is important to ask yourself if a text is biased, because if you are going to assess and evaluate an argument you need to take bias – the speaker's own deeply-held opinions about a subject – into account.

Test yourself 🔊

George Orwell, in his novel *1984*, describes a place where there is no democracy and where the people are ruled by The Party, who constantly churn out biased propaganda. Here, a character is describing what the future will be like under The Party:

> Power is inflicting pain and humiliation. Power is tearing human minds to pieces and putting them together in new shapes of your own choosing ... Progress in our world will be progress towards more pain.

Reread the passage carefully and explain how you know it is biased.

---

58 Recognising inconsistencies

Know the facts 🔊

- **Inconsistencies** occur where an argument has not been carefully thought through: the writer may contradict an earlier point; he/she may also interpret factual information incorrectly and base a key opinion on this misinterpretation; he/she may accept as fact something that is not entirely factual, for example, the results of a flawed survey as highlighted in Unit 55.

Look at the following piece of writing.

> Why is nothing being done about dog dirt in public places such as pavements, parks and local sports grounds? It is not the dogs but the owners who are at fault. How many carry equipment to pick up the dog dirt and dispose of it at home? It is easily acquired in pet shops. How many let the dogs off the lead to run wild? If a dog is caught fouling a public place it should be immediately taken away and destroyed.

Here contradiction is the inconsistency. The writer has claimed that the dogs are not to blame but demands that action is taken against them. No mention is made of penalties for the owners.

Test yourself 🔊

Identify the inconsistency in the following argument.

> Underweight models and film stars are giving out the wrong message to British teenage girls. They are making it seem normal to be seriously and dangerously underweight. Teenagers should take no notice and be themselves. If they want to live on burgers, chips and chocolate bars then they will avoid this danger to their health.

55

56

57

58

59 Identifying implications

Know the facts

- Inconsistencies are not the only problem with arguments that have not been properly thought through. The ideas that writers put forward can often seem sensible and balanced but when they are applied to real life you begin to see how silly or dangerous the writer's ideas can be.

Read the following paragraph.

> Motor cars are a scourge of modern life. They belch out dangerous and obnoxious fumes. They block our town centres making shopping difficult. They are a constant danger to our lives with their high speed. Motor cars should be restricted to one per household. Petrol should be doubled in price to encourage use of public transport. The road tax licence should be doubled and the money spent on the victims of dangerous driving.

Think about the implications of these ideas:

One car per household: Whose car will it be? What will happen if the car owner is away and an emergency journey is needed with no available public transport?

Petrol prices: It is not just car owners who buy petrol. What about the effect on prices through higher delivery charges?

Use of taxes: If this policy was adopted, would money be diverted from education or policing?

The writer has the germ of a good argument. What has not been understood is how complex the whole issue of transport is. The writer has not fully thought out the implication of his/her ideas.

Test yourself

Look at the letters page of any of the national daily papers. Select two or three letters that deal with current controversial issues. Identify the solution put forward by the writer. Now apply it to as many different types of people and situations you can think of. By doing this you are recognising the implications of an argument.

60 Presenting information: headlines

Know the facts

- Effective **headlines** are essential in drawing the attention of the reader to many forms of writing. For example, newspaper headlines draw your attention to the key elements of the article. Front page headlines are especially important as they often help to sell the newspaper. They can be informative, shocking or humorous but above all they must catch the eye and draw attention to the article.

- Similar ideas are used in other writing, such as leaflets selling goods or asking for charitable donations. There is plenty of 'junk mail' around – the writers need to grab attention quickly. They need to sell their double glazing, or get a donation to their good cause – before the reader consigns their work to the litter bin!

- When evaluating the presentation of information look first at the headline. Look at:
  - the size of the printed type. Does this help make an impact?
  - use of colour in the headline
  - the actual words used. Is the phrasing short, snappy and memorable? Is it shocking and memorable? Is it memorable because it asks a question to draw you into the text?

All of these features are used by effective headline writers.

Test yourself

Save all your junk mail for a week. Collect six or so front pages from both tabloid and broadsheet newspapers. Now try to categorise the headlines into different columns. Some column headings could be 'informative', 'dramatic', 'shocking', 'questions', 'witty' (such as a play on words or a biting comment).

Know the facts

Subheadings are used:

- **in longer pieces of writing:** They may 'guide' you through the text in a complex set of facts, such as a chemical process, or in a sophisticated argument, for example the origins of World War II in a history textbook. here other guidance features such as bullet points may also appear. Subheadings may also be used to guide you to the relevant section of a text without your having to reread the whole text.

- **in leaflets:** here subheadings may be used to draw your attention to key aspects of the leaflet, for example the key selling points, the aspect of an appeal which most affects you or the key issues in a campaign directed at somebody like you.

- **to break up the text:** a piece of writing presented as one solid chunk can be forbidding and unattractive. Text is more likely to be read if it is broken into smaller sections by subheadings, bullet points or illustrations.

- In all cases, the use of subheadings and the other features mentioned above is to organise ideas in a piece of writing. This is a vital feature in appealing to the reader.

Test yourself

Find a piece of writing from a school textbook which is written in paragraphs but uses none of the devices mentioned above. Then try to make the text more attractive by breaking it up with subheadings. Think about how the information could be listed rather than written in sentences. When you have finished, check to see if you have 'guided' the reader through the text.

Know the facts

Look out for the following additional features when you read informative texts.

- **Typesetting:** Look out particularly for the use of italics. This may be to highlight a direct quotation. It may also be another way of drawing your attention to a key point in the writing – a key fact, a key selling point or the central point in an argument. Look also for the ways type such as handwriting can suggest informality and friendliness.

- **Underlining or highlighting:** Again, these devices are used to emphasise the key points, issues or ideas in a piece of writing. In a course textbook it may be a key revision point for that topic.

- **Company logos:** Many companies have easily-identifiable logos; think of makes of car or identification marks on clothing. They are there to help you spot immediately that the writing is from, or about, a particular company or its products. We know straight away whether we are interested or to what extent we are interested.

- **Diagrams:** Much of the information we receive can be quite complex or technical. Think of leaflets produced to sell computers, electrical equipment or healthcare. Diagrams, bar charts or pie charts help to present complex information in an easily understandable way.

- **Illustrations:** Pictures do help to break up the text, but they can also affect our feelings. Designers take great care in selecting pictures to accompany text. They are chosen to enhance and support the subject of the writing.

Test yourself

Collect a leaflet from a charitable organisation that asks for a donation, or from a local firm selling I.T. equipment. Identify as many of the above presentational devices as you can. Then write down the effect each device is trying to achieve. Finally, evaluate how successfully you think each device has been used.

63 Persuasive writing

Know the facts

These are trying to persuade you to do something:

– leaflet used in a general election campaign (to persuade you to vote for a particular party)
– advertisement for a new type of shampoo (to encourage you to buy the shampoo)
– article asking for money for a charity (to persuade you to donate some money).

If the texts are successful, the chances are that the writers will have used some of these devices:

- **facts and evidence**

  There are over 1 000 000 members of Amnesty in 150 countries.

- **balanced sentences**

  We don't want starving children to die, we want them to live.

- **sentences which make a direct appeal**

  Go on! Write to your MP!

- **rhetorical questions**

  Don't you want to smell this fresh in the morning?

- **groups of three**

  It is cruel, unfair and barbaric to experiment on animals.

- **repetition of key words or phrases**

  If we act now, one day the world will be clean, one day the sea will be clean, one day the air will be clean.

- **addressing the audience directly**

  It's up to you, today …

When you read a text which is trying to *persuade*, try to identify how the writer appeals to the reader.

Test yourself

Which devices have been used here to appeal to the audience?

(a) Friends, Romans, countrymen, lend me your ears.

(b) Nibble them in the morning, nobble them in the evening.

(c) Act now, before it's too late!

64 Emotive writing

Know the facts

- Another way in which writers might appeal to their audience is by using **emotive language** – language which plays on your emotions and feelings.

Read these two sentences:

> In the war, 300 children were made homeless.
>
> In the terrifying war, 300 innocent, defenceless children were suddenly made homeless.

The second sentence contains only four more words than the first, but is far more powerful. *Terrifying* emphasises the horror of the fighting, *innocent* and *defenceless* stress that the children themselves were innocent victims of the conflict, and *suddenly* reminds us of the unpredictable nature of war. We are far more likely to want to read on (to find out what happened to the children, for example) because our emotions have been touched.

- Look carefully at the **adjectives** and **adverbs** used in a text: these provide good clues as to whether the writing is emotive or not.

- The writer's choice of **nouns** and **verbs** may also be important in creating an emotive piece. Think about the difference between 'The fire burnt down their house' and 'The fire wrecked their home'. (Look at Unit 92, Atmosphere, for more on this.)

Test yourself

Add a variety of adjectives and adverbs to these sentences to make them more emotive.

1 The _____ gunman fired on the _____ girl.

   (for example, The <u>vicious</u> gunman fired on the <u>defenceless</u> girl.)

2 The _____ dog ran along the _____ beach.

3 The _____ doctor acted _____ to save her life.

4 The _____ British countryside is being _____ ruined.

65 Selecting material appropriate to purpose

Know the facts

Generally we can identify the type of writing in front of us merely by looking. Think of the principal features of these types of writing:

- the front page of a tabloid newspaper
- the front page of a quality newspaper
- the letters page of a teenage magazine
- a full page advert for a foreign holiday
- a flyer through the letterbox for a new local video rental outlet
- a page in a dictionary
- a page in a geography textbook.

- We can recognise all of these publications very quickly from their appearance. They all contain features that are essential to their purpose. For example, the advert for a foreign holiday may well feature exotic-looking locations and a comparison of prices; the geography textbook may feature diagrams, statistical evidence and lists of key features.

- The writers and designers have the purposes clearly in their minds when they publish the text. Remember this when you are looking at a variety of different types of text on a common theme. Ask yourself: Why has the writer chosen to give me the information in this way? Where would I normally find this type of text? What is the subject matter? Who would normally read this type of text? All these questions will help you to work out the purpose of the writing.

Test yourself

Look again at the list of texts above. Write down the features that are essential to the purpose of each one (the advert and the geography text book have been done) for you. Use the question steps above to help you.

66 Collating material

Know the facts

- There are many parts of examination preparation where you might need to look at texts or parts of texts in some detail.

- You may be given a set of texts on a linked theme – homelessness, drug abuse or truancy – and you will need to pull information from these texts. This will help you to see similarities and differences and to see the whole picture.

- Most students use notetaking skills here, and there are almost as many ways of making notes as there are students. What is essential, no matter what your method, is that your notes should be suited to their purpose. Notes for revision need to be clear and comprehensive; notes made in an exam need to be just enough for you to plan your way through that particular question.

- If you are collating information then your notes should highlight the details of different texts. Your final notes should show how these details fit together, either in agreement or on different sides of the fence.

Test yourself

Collect together an article from a newspaper, a leaflet and a page from a reference source on a similar theme such as homelessness, drug abuse or truancy. Try looking on the Internet too. Make notes on the details given in each text and collate them so you can fit together and describe the differing opinions they express.

67 Rhythm

Know the facts

- **Rhythm** is the 'beat' of a poem or piece of prose. A regular rhythm can help to provide a framework for the writing, but it also helps to establish the mood.

Read this excerpt from the start of John Keats's poem 'To Autumn' aloud:

> Season of mists and mellow fruitfulness,
> Close bosom-friend of the maturing sun;
> Conspiring with him how to load and bless
> With fruit the vines that round the thatch-eaves run;

Can you hear the gentle beat that flows with the words? It helps to suggest the languid, sleepy atmosphere being described.

In 'In Memory of W.B. Yeats' by W.H. Auden, the rhythm is quite different. Read it aloud:

> Earth, receive an honoured guest;
> William Yeats is laid to rest.

The strong beat suggests a military march and that the funeral being described is very formal.

- In your exam, you could underline the syllables where the beat falls in a text, like this:

> and <u>bless</u>
> With <u>fruit</u> the <u>vines</u> that <u>round</u> the <u>thatch</u>-eaves <u>run</u>

- Remember, there is no point is commenting on the rhythm if you don't explain how it adds to the mood of the poem.

Test yourself

For each of these lines, mark in the beats and suggest the type of mood that the rhythm creates:

1 Half a league, half a league, half a league onward
'The Charge of the Light Brigade'
by Alfred, Lord Tennyson

2 Up and down, up and down,
They go, the gray rat, and the brown.
'After the Salvo' by H.H. Asquith

68 Rhyme

Know the facts

- A **rhyme**, of course, is when the sound at the end of one word matches the sound at the end of a nearby word. Everyone can tell you that 'rain in Spain stays mainly on the plain' – the rhyming words have helped to make the line memorable.

- Rhyme is used by poets and authors to do more than simply help us remember what they have written, though. Simon Armitage's 'Poem' is full of rhyming lines:

> And for his mum he hired a private nurse.
> And every Sunday taxied her to church.
> And he blubbed when she went from bad to worse.
> And twice he lifted ten quid from her purse.

Think about the effect that the rhymes have. The simple, ordinary rhymes reflect the simple, ordinary life of the man who is being described.

The shock of the last line (the fact that he stole from his mother when he was usually so considerate towards her) is emphasised because of the rhyme – we *expected* the rhyme word to describe another good thing that he did, but it does just the opposite.

- **Sight rhyme** is when a pair of words look as if they should rhyme but don't – *cough* and *through*, for example.

- **Internal rhyme** is when the sound is repeated within lines of poetry, not just at the end.

Test yourself

Comment on the effectiveness of the rhymes in 'In Flanders Fields' by John McCrae.

> In Flanders Fields the poppies blow
> Beneath the crosses, row on row
> That mark our place; and in the sky
> The larks, still bravely singing, fly
> Scarce heard amid the guns below.

69 Similes

Know the facts 📜

- **Similes** are comparisons. Writers use similes to help you imagine certain images and feelings. Think about your own writing or talking. If you are trying to describe a sight or feeling to a friend that is outside their experience then you often do it by making a comparison with something they do recognise.

- When using a simile a writer simply says that something is **like**, or **as**, something else:

> This City now doth, like a garment, wear
> The beauty of the morning;

> a black-
> Back gull bent like an iron bar slowly.

- Both of the above are examples of similes. However, in coursework writing or in an exam it is not enough just to identify similes. You need to say how effective they are; what the writer is trying to help you imagine and whether they have achieved this.

- The first example above is from William Wordsworth's poem, 'Composed Upon Westminster Bridge'. Wordsworth is asking you to imagine that the City is a woman who puts on a beautiful dress (a garment) which enhances her own beauty. The second example is from Ted Hughes's poem, 'Wind'. Here he is asking you to imagine the strength of the wind as the bird in flight is gradually pushed back by it. You need to decide for yourself how well the writers have succeeded in describing a beautiful morning and a strong wind in these examples.

Test yourself 📜

Explain whether you find these similes effective:

> 1 I have seen old ships sail like swans asleep ...
> J.E. Flecker
>
> 2 And then the whining school-boy, with his satchel,
> And shining morning face, creeping like snail
> Unwillingly to school.
>
> William Shakespeare

70 Metaphors

Know the facts 📜

- A **metaphor** is also a form of comparison but asks you to use your imagination more completely than a simile. Here the writer says that something actually is something else and asks you to imagine the features of the comparison.

Look at this metaphor at the start of 'The Sea' by James Reeves:

> The sea is a hungry dog,
> Giant and grey,
> He rolls on the beach all day.

Here the poet is asking us to imagine the incoming sea 'eating up' the beach like a hungry dog desperately searching for food and then devouring it. In this example the metaphor is quite clear in the first line.

- It is important not just to identify the metaphor. You must say how the poet is asking you to use your imagination and whether or not you think the metaphor is successful.

Test yourself 📜

Pick out the simile and the metaphor in the following extract from 'Nightride' by Gillian Clarke. What is the writer asking you to imagine? How effective are these comparisons?

> The road unwinding under our wheels
> New in the headlamps like a roll of foil.
> The rain is a recorder writing tunes
> In telegraph wires, kerbs and cats' eyes,
> Reflections and the lights of little towns.

71 Personification

Know the facts

- **Personification** is a type of metaphor in which the writer gives human qualities and feelings to non-human things. One of the most common examples is how writers treat the seasons of the year. They often see them as human beings in various ages: the youth of Spring, the full grown person in Summer, maturity in Autumn and old age in Winter.

- Again it is vital not just to identify the personification but to write about how it works on the reader's imagination. Look at the opening lines of Gillian Clarke's poem 'Miracle on St David's Day':

> An afternoon yellow and open-mouthed
> with daffodils. The sun treads the path
> among cedars and enormous oaks.

'Open-mouthed' reminds the reader of the shape of the trumpet of the daffodil; 'treads' suggests an image of the sunlight making its way across the ground. These are the writer's intentions; do they work for you?

Test yourself

Identify the personification in the following lines from 'Porphyria's Lover' by Robert Browning. What scene do they suggest to you? Are they effective in creating a picture of a stormy night?

> The rain set early in to-night,
> The sullen wind was soon awake,
> It tore the elm-tops down for spite,
> And did its worst to vex the lake:

72 Alliteration

Know the facts

- **Alliteration** is the deliberate repetition of consonant sounds at the beginning of words close to each other.

- The writer may be trying to draw attention to those words, or may be using hard or soft sounds for particular effects.

Here are some examples:

James Reeves wrote about walking through 'Beech Leaves' with a 'crisp and crashing sound.' Here the use of the hard *c*'s adds to the picture of the dried and crunchy autumn leaves.

Writing about 'Snow In The Suburbs', Thomas Hardy wrote, 'there is no waft of wind with the fleecy fall.' The soft *w*'s and *f*'s give the impression of the soft covering of snow on the ground.

Wilfred Owen, a poet writing in World War I, talked about 'the stuttering rifles' rapid rattle' in 'Anthem for Doomed Youth'. The awkwardness of the repeated *r*'s echoes the sound of the jerky firing of the guns.

- Alliteration is not only effective in poetry, though. It is often found in prose, to create similar effects to those mentioned above.

- Advertisers make a lot of use of alliteration, too! It can help us to remember the name of a product. Think of 'P-p-p pick up a Penguin' and 'A finger of Fudge'.

Test yourself

1 Read the extract below and identify the alliterative sounds.

> And tinkling trees ice-bound,
> Changed into weeping willows, sweep the ground.
> 'Hard Frost' by Andrew Young

2 Explain how the alliterative words add to the effectiveness of the lines. Compare your ideas to those in the answers section at the back of the book.

3 Now write a few lines describing your classroom at school, involving alliteration.

73 Assonance, consonance and sibilance

Know the facts

These are ways of linking words in a pattern of sounds and are particularly effective when poetry is read aloud:

- **Assonance** is the repetition of similar vowel sounds either in words close together in the writing or in different syllables in the same word. At the start of his poem 'Exposure', Wilfred Owen, a World War I poet, writes:

> Our brains ache, in the merciless iced east winds that knive us ...

Here, the assonance created using the *i* sounds gives the impression of the swish of a cutting wind and helps the reader to appreciate the horrific cold that the soldiers had to endure. The wind itself is their enemy here, driving into them even more piercingly than an enemy's bayonet.

- **Consonance** is the repetition of similar-sounding consonants. Here, in the poem 'Exposure', Owen is describing exhausted men going back to their base after battle:

> Slowly our ghosts drag home ...

- **Sibilance** is the repetition of *s* sounds. Again in 'Exposure', Owen describes men under attack from enemy gunfire:

> Sudden successive flights of bullets streak the silence.

Test yourself

1 Explain the effect of the consonance in the line from 'Exposure'.

2 Explain the effect of the sibilance in the line from 'Exposure'.

74 Onomatopoeia

Know the facts

- **Onomatopoeia** is when a word sounds like the noise it is describing. Everyday speech is full of common examples:

> the *whoosh* of the washing machine
>
> the *buzzing* of the bees
>
> the *clatter* of pots and pans
>
> the bubble *popped.*

- Onomatopoeia can be used very effectively in prose or poetry when the author is trying to build up an impression of sound.

Wilfred Owen, in his World War I poem 'Dulce et decorum est', describes how he could hear the blood 'come gargling from the froth-corrupted lungs' of a soldier who had been injured in a gas attack. The word *gargling* suggests the horrible bubbly sound perfectly.

In Thomas Hardy's short story *The Withered Arm*, there is a discussion between the workers in the milkshed:

> The discussion waxed so warm that the purr of the milk streams became jerky.

The word *purr* suggests a smooth, gentle humming noise as the milkers filled their pails. (It was interrupted when the milkers got so excited about what they were talking about that they lost concentration on their job!)

71 72 73 74

Test yourself

1 Underline the onomatopoeic words in this extract from a poem by Ted Hughes called 'Tractor':

> The starting lever
> Cracks its action, like a snapping knuckle.
>
> I squirt commercial sure-fire
> Down the black throat – it just coughs.

2 What is the effect of the onomatopoeic words? Do they help you to imagine the difficulty the man had in starting his tractor on a cold day?

75 Hyperbole

Know the facts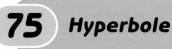

- **Hyperbole** is deliberate exaggeration for effect. You do it yourself in speech when you say 'I'm starving' when you are mildly hungry, or 'It's freezing' when it is slightly cool outside.

Thomas Hood used this device when describing a foggy day in 'November':

> No sun, no moon,
> No morn, no noon,
> No dawn, no dusk, no proper time of day.

Of course, the sun and the moon *did* exist and the clock could have told him when it was morning and noon, but the day *felt* completely empty and colourless and changeless. In this example, **repetition** is also effective in conveying the monotony of the November day. The poet can't seem to be able to vary his phrasing: each clause begins 'No ...'.

Test yourself

1 A gargoyle is a stone gutter outlet in medieval plumbing. They can be seen on the outside of old churches, up under the eaves. They are often carved into fantastic faces and creatures.

   Underline the hyperbole in this example:

> Gargoyles, grey and terrifying,
> Spilling an ocean from their gaping jaws.
>
> *'Ile de la Cite'* by Jim McRae

2 Explain why the hyperbole is effective. Compare your ideas to those in the answers section at the back of the book.

76 Repetition

Know the facts

- Repetition is often used by writers to:
  - emphasise a point or idea
  - add to the sound and rhythm of their writing.

Look at these lines from Andre Voznesensky's poem 'First Ice', which make use of both effects of repetition:

> She'll have to go home, alone,
> Along the icy street.
>
> First ice. It is the first time.
> The first ice of telephone phrases.
>
> Frozen tears glitter on her cheeks –
> The first ice of human hurt.

- Both words of the title, *first* and *ice*, are repeated frequently throughout the poem. The repetition helps you to see all the different shades of meaning that the words could have.

It is <u>icy</u> cold weather, the street is <u>icy</u> and slippery for the <u>first</u> time this winter. She hears <u>icy</u> words on the telephone for the <u>first</u> time ever (perhaps from her boyfriend – or now former boyfriend?) and her heart feels <u>icy</u> for the <u>first</u> time – she's cold and lonely and unloved.

The repetition emphasises her sad situation and makes you sympathise with her. It also gives an echo-like quality to the poem that makes it more enjoyable to read.

Test yourself

Identify the repetition in this passage from Charlotte Bronte's *Jane Eyre*. Little Jane is sent to the red-room as a punishment.

> The red-room was a spare chamber very seldom slept in ... A bed supported on massive pillars of mahogany, hung with curtains of deep red damask, stood ... in the centre; the two large windows, with their blinds always drawn down, were half shrouded in festoons and falls of similar drapery; the carpet was red.

How does the repetition add to the effectiveness of the extract?

Know the facts

In writing, irony is often used to add humour, but it can be used to make serious points too. There are two basic kinds of irony.

Verbal irony

Irony occurs if a person says one thing and means another.

- We use irony quite often: how many times have you heard someone say to you, 'Lovely day, isn't it?' if it is pouring with rain?

- *Pride and Prejudice* by Jane Austen opens, *It is a truth universally acknowledged, that a single man, in possession of a good fortune, must be in want of a wife.* It is not a truth, of course, but Mrs Bennet, who has five daughters to get married off, is keen to grasp it when an eligible man moves into the area!

Irony of situation

In this case, something is ironic if an event happens that, by coincidence, has an interesting or strange effect on another event. Here are two examples:

- A man may be thinking how hilarious it is that his friend's daughter had run away to get married, while at the same time his own daughter is in the process of running away to get married without her father's knowledge.

- In Thomas Hardy's *A Withered Arm*, a woman needs the blood of a recently-hanged man to rid herself of a curse. She does not know that the hanged man in question is her husband's illegitimate son.

Test yourself

Here is an excerpt from the start of Dickens's *Great Expectations*. Pip's parents have died and are buried in the churchyard. One day, as Pip is visiting the grave, he meets an escaped convict. Pip is terrified.

> 'Now then, lookee here!' said the man. 'Where's you mother?'
> 'There, sir!' said I.
> He started, made a short run, and stopped and looked over his shoulder.
> 'There, sir!' I timidly exclaimed. '"Also Georgina".
> That's my mother.'

Why is this ironic? What is the effect?

Know the facts

Look at these lines from William Shakespeare's *Othello*:

Othello is praising his General, Iago:

> A man he is of honesty and trust.

Yet here we see Iago speaking:

> Divinity of hell!
> When devils will their blackest sins put on,
> They do suggest at first with heavenly shows,
> As I do now:
>
> I'll pour this pestilence into his [Othello's] ear

- Iago's words are to do with hell and poison. We associate hell with evil, so his words let the audience know that Iago is an evil and poisonous character. Othello and other characters don't find out until it is too late, but we, the audience, know all along. When the audience know something significant that the characters in a drama don't, it is called **dramatic irony**. Dramatic irony adds suspense to a play.

Test yourself

J.B. Priestley set his play *An Inspector Calls* in 1912, but he wrote it in 1945. In it, Mr Birling boasts:

> I say there isn't a chance of war. The world's developing so fast it'll make war impossible ... And then ships. Why, a friend of mine went over this new liner last week – the Titanic – she sails next week ... every luxury – and unsinkable, absolutely unsinkable.

Identify the dramatic irony in this passage. What does it tell us about Mr Birling?

75
76
77
78

79 Narrators

Know the facts

Third person

Most prose texts, whether fiction or non-fiction, are written in the third person. This means that the writer is not personally involved in the writing. People in the story are referred to as *he* or *she* (not *you* or *I*). The advantages of writing in the third person are that the writer:

- knows everything that is happening to everyone
- can act as a reporter
- may be unbiased
- may allow you to 'read the minds' of their characters.

First person

Many prose texts, particularly novels, are written in the first person. The writer takes on the role of one of the characters in the story and so refers to that character as *I*. The text may be written in the form of a diary. The advantages of writing in the first person are:

- the audience knows the character's thoughts and feelings exactly, so you feel very close to them
- you see things and experience things only through the character's eyes.

- Sometimes a writer switches between different voices within a text to make the most of all these advantages.

Test yourself

Here are extracts from two novels. Identify which narrative voice the writer has used.

> (a) I said one Hail Mary and four Our Fathers, because I preferred the Our Fathers to the Hail Mary and it was longer and better. I said them to myself in the shed in the dark.
>
> *Paddy Clarke Ha Ha Ha* by Roddy Doyle
>
> (b) The doctor refilled his pipe ... He listened to Pelagia clattering outdoors in the yard.
>
> *Captain Corelli's Mandolin* by Louis de Bernieres

80 Prose: character

Know the facts

- You would only gain a few marks by supplying an account of the content of a text as the main part of your exam answer. You need to go beyond simply showing that you understand the story.

- Concentrate on the language the writer has used to present a character. What do you learn from the language about the qualities of that character?

Look at this description of the character Mrs Joe from Charles Dickens' *Great Expectations*.

> My sister, Mrs. Joe, with *black* hair and eyes, had such a prevailing *redness of skin* that I sometimes used to wonder whether it was possible she washed herself with a *nutmeg-grater* instead of soap. She was *tall and bony*, and almost always wore a *coarse* apron, fastened over her figure behind with two loops, and having a square *impregnable* bib in front, that was stuck full of *pins and needles*.

Earlier Dickens had described Mr Joe as *mild, good-natured, sweet-tempered, easy-going*. Now look at the words in italics. They present a woman who is raw, harsh, and difficult to approach in contrast to her husband.

- Looking carefully at the words used will help you to gain an insight into Mrs Joe's character.

Test yourself

Look at this description of Miss Murdstone from Dickens's *David Copperfield*. Identify the words that give you an insight into her character.

> She brought with her, two uncompromising hard black boxes, with her initials on the lids in hard brass nails. When she paid the coachman she took her money out of a hard steel purse, and she kept the purse in a very jail of a bag which hung upon her arm by a heavy chain, and shut up like a bite. I had never, at that time, seen such a metallic lady altogether as Miss Murdstone was.

Know the facts

- When you read a text you are aware that the writer is trying to arouse certain feelings. The writer may want you to:
  - share their emotions, such as love or anger
  - share their feelings about aspects of the world
  - share their feelings about aspects of a world we may have lost.

The setting of a work may help to do this.

Look at this extract from *Hard Times* by Charles Dickens about the fictional town of Coketown at the height of the Industrial Revolution in the nineteenth century.

> It was a town of *red* brick, or of brick that would have been red if the *smoke* and *ashes* had allowed it; but as matters stood it was a town of *unnatural red* and *black* like the *painted face of a savage*. It was a town of machinery and tall chimneys, out of which *interminable serpents of smoke* trailed themselves for ever and ever, and *never got uncoiled.*

- The words in italics give an impression of savagery and evil. Dickens goes on to describe dirt and noise. He was trying to convey his feeling that industrialisation in the Industrial Revolution led to a decay in people's lives.

Test yourself

Look at this extract from *Bleak House*, another of Dickens' novels. He is describing the landscape around Temple Bar and the High Court.

> Fog everywhere. Fog up the river, where it flows among green aits and meadows; fog down the river, where it rolls defiled among the tiers of shipping, and the waterside pollutions of a great (and dirty) city. The raw afternoon is rawest, and the dense fog is densest, and the muddy streets are muddiest, near ... Temple Bar.

Identify the words which you think show Dickens's attitude to the legal profession.

Know the facts

- The nature of the poetic style of writing often means that a lot of ideas are packed into a few words, so you may need to read a poem more times, and more carefully, than a section of prose to understand it. However, you can approach a poem in exactly the same way as you approach a piece of prose.

- Poets give clues about the characters in their poems as prose writers do:

> My father *worked* with a horse-plough,
> His *shoulders globed like a full sail strung*
> Between the shafts and the furrow.
> The horses *strained* at his clicking tongue.
>
> An **expert**. He would **set the wing**
> And **fit the bright steel-pointed sock**.
> The sod rolled over without breaking.
> At the headrig, with **a single pluck**
>
> Of reins, the *sweating* team turned round
> And back into the land. His eye
> Narrowed and angled at the ground,
> Mapping the furrow exactly.
>
> 'Follower' by Seamus Heaney

- Look at the words in italics. Heaney is trying to build the picture of a strong man involved in strenuous activity. However, this work is not just heavy, it needs control and accuracy – the bold words suggest this. The technical terms also build up a picture of skill as well as power.

Test yourself

1 Read the opening lines of Wilfred Owen's poem 'Dulce et decorum est':

> Bent double, like old beggars under sacks,
> Knock-kneed, coughing like hags, we cursed through sludge,

Identify the words which help you engage with the situation of the troops. What effect do these words create?

79
80
81
82

Know the facts

- Poets, as well as prose writers, may also use descriptions of settings to show us their attitude towards something they feel strongly about.

Edward Thomas was a poet at the time of World War One. Many of his poems look back to the glories of the English countryside in the years before 1914. Look at the last two verses from his poem 'Adlestrop'. Look at how the details of the writing help you to engage with his feelings of nostalgia.

> And willows, willow-herb, and grass,
> And meadowsweet, and haycocks dry,

(These are simple plants, suggesting life *once* seemed simple to Thomas.)

> No whit less still and lonely fair
> Than the high cloudlets in the sky.

(This suggests peace, calm and tranquility.)

> And for that minute a blackbird sang
>
> Close by, and round him, mistier,
> Farther and farther, all the birds
> of Oxfordshire and Gloucestershire.

(... until other birds join in the chorus. The pure sound swells around him, in contrast to the harsh noise he usually hears.)

- Thomas does not need to explain directly to us that he regrets the passing of the old ways – the language in his poem conveys his attitude clearly.

Test yourself

Look at this verse from Thomas Hardy's poem 'The Darkling Thrush'. He wrote it at the end of the nineteenth century, as the century was dying away. Identify the words which suggest the idea of dying away.

> The land's sharp features seemed to be
> The Century's corpse outleant,
> His crypt the cloudy canopy
> The wind his death lament.
> The ancient pulse of germ and birth
> Was shrunken hard and dry,
> And every spirit upon earth
> Seemed fervourless as I.

Know the facts

- As a drama is made up entirely of speech, in a play you cannot learn about a character from a writer's description; you need to decide what a character is like from:
  — what they say
  — what they do.

What characters say

Lady Macbeth, on realising that she will have the chance to become queen if she can persuade her husband to kill the current king, says:

> Come, you spirits
> That tend on mortal thoughts, unsex me here;
> And fill me, from the crown to the toe, top-full
> Of direst cruelty!

Her words reveal her to be ambitious, brave and willing to go to great lengths to achieve her goal.

What characters do

What the characters in J.B. Priestley's play *An Inspector Calls* do marks them out just as clearly:

> **Birling:** You didn't just come here to see me, then?
> **Inspector:** No.
>
> *The other four exchange bewildered and perturbed glances.*

The confusion and possible guilt of the four characters is now obvious to the audience – they didn't have to *say* anything: those glances were enough.

Test yourself

What do you learn about Barbara in this excerpt?

> **Barbara:** That's right, Bill. Hold out against it. Put out your strength. Don't let's get you cheap. Todger Farimile said that he wrestled for three nights against his salvation harder than he ever wrestled with the Jap at the music hall.
>
> *Major Barbara* by George Bernard Shaw

Know the facts

You also learn about key characters from what other characters reveal.

Look at these lines from *Macbeth*. Here a sergeant is reporting Macbeth's actions at the vital point of a battle. The audience has not yet seen Macbeth.

> For brave Macbeth – well he deserves that name –
> Disdaining Fortune, with his brandish'd steel
> Which smoked with bloody execution,
> Like valour's minion, carv'd out his passage
> Till he faced the slave;
> Which ne'er shook hands, nor bade farewell to him,
> Till he unseam'd him from the nave to th'chaps,
> And fix'd his head upon our battlements.

- We know a lot about Macbeth before we have even met him. We could say:
  — he is brave and fearless (and is admired by others for being so)
  — he is not afraid to do bloody deeds
  — he is loyal to his cause.

Part of the audience's interest in meeting Macbeth will be to see how he lives up to their expectations after this build up!

Test yourself

In contrast, here is a section from a modern play, 'Death of a Salesman', by Arthur Miller. Linda is the wife of Willy.

> **Linda:** I don't say he's a great man. Willy Loman never made a lot of money. His name was never in the paper. He's not the finest character that ever lived. But he's a human being, and a terrible thing is happening to him. So attention must be paid. He's not to be allowed to fall into his grave like an old dog. Attention, attention must be paid to such a person.

What do we learn about Willy? Think about what we discover from Linda's words.

83

84

85

Know the facts

- In a play, just as in prose and poetry, it is important for the writer to set the scene, not only so that the action that unfolds on the stage is as real as possible, but to give insight into the drama.

- Some playwrights describe a set in a lot of detail. For example, the set at the opening of *An Inspector Calls* is described quite specifically by J.B. Priestley:

> The dining room of a fairly large suburban house ... It has good solid furniture of the period. The general effect is substantial and heavily comfortable, not cosy and homelike ... The lighting should be pink and intimate until the Inspector arrives ...

- This description gives information about the family – they are obviously proud of their dining room; the pink light suggests a warm atmosphere.

- Shakespeare, though, did not have access to the elaborate stage sets of today and so his characters helped the audience imagine themselves in the environment of the play.

> Suppose within the girdle of these walls
> Are now confined two mighty monarchies,
> Whose high upreared and abutting fronts
> The perilous narrow ocean parts assunder.
>
> *King Henry V*

This description helps place the play in the tense royal courts of England and France before a battle.

Test yourself

What do you think J.M. Synge is telling us about the situation in his play *The Playboy of the Western World* from the way that one character describes the setting?

> I stood a while outside ... and I could hear the cows breathing and sighing in the stillness of the air, and not a step moving any place from this gate to the bridge.

87 Shakespeare: blank verse

Know the facts

- Most of Shakespeare's plays are written in what is called blank verse. Basically, this tells you about the rhythm of the lines. Shakespeare often used blank verse as it is the form of rhythm which comes closest to natural speech. The rhythm provides a framework for the language to hang on.

- Blank verse is composed of lines called **iambic pentameters**. An **iamb** is an unstressed syllable followed by a stressed syllable. The word *Macbeth* is a good example. If you say it aloud, the *beth* part is emphasised more than the *Mac* part. Five iambs in a row make an iambic pentameter (*pent* means 'five' in Greek).

This example of a perfect iambic pentameter is from *Macbeth*:

> To <u>know</u> / my <u>deed</u>, / 'twere <u>best</u> / not <u>know</u> / my<u>self</u>.

(Do remember, though, that not *every* line in Shakespeare is an exact iambic pentameter, because that would sound very stilted.)

- If you want to mention iambic feet in your exam, remember it is only worthwhile if you explain why their use is significant in adding to the atmosphere of the scene.

Test yourself

What is the effect of the blank verse in the example above? Answer *true* or *false*.

1 The stressed words are important, so the audience can feel Macbeth's emotion more clearly.

2 The force of his feeling is emphasised.

3 It makes Macbeth sound comic.

88 Shakespeare: rhyme

Know the facts

- Blank verse does not usually rhyme, just as our everyday speech does not usually rhyme, but Shakespeare does use rhyme to great effect in some cases. If you spot a rhyme in one of Shakespeare's plays, it's usually there for a particular reason:

- **To emphasise a key point in the drama:** Often to round off a scene, for example, when *Macbeth* has finally decided to murder the king, he says:

> Away, and mock the time with fairest show
> False face must hide what the false heart doth
> know.

- **To tell us something about certain characters:** The witches in *Macbeth* speak in rhyming couplets which helps to identify them as different from the other characters – and certainly as suspicious!

> Fillet of a fenny snake,
> In the cauldron boil and bake;
> Eye of newt and toe of frog,
> Wool of bat and tongue of dog ...

- **To emphasise the relationship between characters:** Romeo and Juliet slip naturally into a sonnet when they first meet, which proves to the audience that they are made for each other:

> **Romeo:** Have not saints lips, and holy palmers too?
> **Juliet:** Ay, pilgrim, lips that they must use in prayer.
> **Romeo:** O then, dear saint, let lips do what hands so:
> Then pray, grant thou, lest faith turn to
> despair.

Test yourself

Look carefully at the play you are studying to see if you can find any rhyme. Can you think of some reasons why Shakespeare used rhyme at that particular point?

89 Shakespeare: prose

Know the facts

- Blank verse emphasises the high standing of a character. Shakespeare's audiences knew that only somebody of good birth could speak so poetically.

- So, the only time Shakespeare does not use poetry in his plays, and writes in prose instead, is when he is writing about the 'low' or comic characters. Unlike the rich nobles who are the main characters, these are usually servants or poor people. Often their language is fairly bawdy, too! Elizabethan audiences would have enjoyed the rude jokes that they made.

In *Macbeth*, the drunken porter always raises a laugh:

> *Knock, knock, knock:* Who's there, I' the name of Beelzebub?

That is *not* the politest way to open the door to one of your master's guests!

- Mercutio speaks in prose in *Romeo and Juliet* which emphasises his bawdy jokes and puns, and proves to us that he is 'a bit of a lad':

> **Benvolio:** Here comes Romeo, here comes Romeo.
> **Mercutio:** Without his roe, like a dried herring: O flesh, flesh, how art thou finished!

Test yourself

What impression do we get of Sir Toby Belch in this passage from *Twelfth Night?*

> These clothes are good enough to drink in, and so be these boots too; and they be not, let them hang themselves by their own straps.

Note down some ideas and compare your ideas to those on the Answers page.

86
87
88
89

Know the facts

- **Dialect** is a version of a language that has its own distinctive grammar, accent and vocabulary. A dialect is spoken by a group of people with their own particular culture.

- In the second line of 'Old Father' by John Boatswain (see Unit 91), it is interesting that *cold* (noun) and *bite* (verb) do not agree as they would in formal English. Here the writer is deliberately using the Caribbean dialect. This style of language helps to convince you that the writer has experienced these problems and that everything is new to him – just as his style of language may be new to people who have not come across Caribbean people before.

Read this start of a poem in dialect.

> this is thi
>
> six a clock
>
> news thi
>
> man said n
>
> thi reason
>
> a talk wia
>
> BBC accent
>
> iz coz yi
>
> widny wahnt
>
> mi ti talk
>
> aboot thi
>
> trooth wia
>
> voice lik
>
> wanna yoo
>
> scruff.

The poem is 'Unrelated Incidents'. It is by Tom Leonard, a Scots poet who writes in a Glaswegian dialect.

The reasons why his use of dialect here is so effective are:

- the poem seems to be spoken by a BBC newsreader

- S/he explains why the BBC thinks it is important to read the news in a 'BBC accent'– nobody will take the news seriously if it's read with a 'voice lik wanna yoo scruff'.

It is not that simple, though ...

- S/he speaks here in the dialect of an ordinary viewer – exactly the kind of voice the newsreader is rejecting.

- A newsreader would never really reveal his/her prejudices directly to the viewer in this way. So what the newsreader 'says' in this poem perhaps needs to be seen as the *unspoken* message (or subtext) of the way the news is presented. If the poem was written in standard English, the message would not be so striking.

Test yourself

This is the start of a poem called 'Half Caste'.

> Explain yuself
>
> wha yu mean
>
> when yu say half-caste
>
> yu mean when picasso
>
> mix red an green
>
> is a half-caste canvas
>
> John Agard, *NEAB Anthology*

1 Rewrite these lines in standard English.

2 What do you think is the poet's message?

Know the facts

- You need to show that you can recognise how the text tells you about a different **lifestyle**. This difference may be because the text tells you about a different period in history or about life in a country where the conditions of life are different to your own.

Look at the opening lines of Hugh Boatswain's poem 'Old Father':

> Old Father to England in Winter '59.
> Cold bite him hard,
> Make him bawl in his small basement room
> By the Grove.

By examining the poem carefully you can begin to appreciate what life was like for Caribbean immigrants to Britain in the 1950s. Here are some of the clues that suggest his father is from a different culture.

- The opening line is in the form of a short statement giving the time and place.
- The language of the poem reflects the speech of some early immigrants.
- The capital *F* for *Father* indicates more formal respect for parents than in England.
- The second line has the personification of *bite*, suggesting that the cold weather was particularly painful to the new immigrant from a warmer climate.
- In the third line, *bawl* is a word we often use of crying babies. This adds to the effect of pain in the second line and gives the picture of someone dependent on others in an alien world.

Test yourself

What do these lines tell you about life where there is insufficient water?

> The municipal pipe bursts,
> Silver crashes to the ground
> and the flow has found
> a roar of tongues.
>   From 'Blessing' by Imtiaz Dharker, *NEAB Anthology*

1 Why is it significant that water is seen as silver?

2 What might the roar of tongues be?

92 Atmosphere

Know the facts

> The following Thursday was changeable, damp and gloomy; and the night threatened to be windy and unpleasant.
>   *The Distracted Preacher* by Thomas Hardy

- The **atmosphere**, or mood, of this passage is undoubtedly grey and dull. We know that something far more serious – and, perhaps, frightening – is about to happen. Hardy has set the scene for us by creating an effective atmosphere. He does so by using lots of doom-laden adjectives: *changeable, damp, gloomy, windy, unpleasant*.

In the section on emotive writing (Unit 64), you looked at these two sentences:

> The fire burnt down their house.

> The fire wrecked their home.

- Both sentences contain the same basic information, but the second is more emotive and has a more vivid atmosphere. *Home* appeals to our emotions more than *house* because a house is simply somewhere to live, while a home is somewhere warm and safe; similarly, *wrecked* is a more dramatic word than *burnt down*.

- *Any* type of word (noun, verb, adjective, adverb) can contribute to a text's atmosphere. As you read, try to see whether a pattern is emerging that signals the mood the writer is trying to create.

Test yourself

The two lines of script below are very boring and lack atmosphere. Add details to each one to create:

(a) a scary atmosphere

(b) a happy, relaxed atmosphere.

> 'Hello John,' said Jane.

> 'Hello Jane,' said John. 'Fancy meeting you here.'

For example, a scary atmosphere has been created here:

> 'Hello John,' breathed Jane.

> 'Hello Jane,' whispered John, and laughed harshly. 'Fancy meeting you here.'

93 Vocabulary: the five senses

Know the facts

- One of the ways in which both poets and prose writers can make their writing more vivid is to use words that appeal to your *senses*. You are able to imagine things much more clearly if you can virtually see, hear, smell, touch and taste what is being described.

For example, Charles Dickens, in *The Pickwick Papers*, describes the month of August:

> August comes when we remember nothing but clear skies, green fields, and <u>sweet-smelling</u> flowers ... Orchards and cornfields <u>ring with the hum</u> of labour; trees bend beneath the <u>thick clusters of rich fruit</u> which bow their branches to the ground; and the corn, piled in graceful sheaves, ... tinges the landscape with a <u>golden hue</u>.

He paints the picture so richly with scents, sounds, juicy tastes and colours that you feel you are there: the sensory language enables you to share in the scene. In your own reading, see how often you can spot a writer *appealing to your senses* to make the writing more real.

Test yourself

The short poem below, 'Autumn', was written by T.E. Hulme. Identify the words and phrases that appeal to your senses.

> A touch of cold in the Autumn night –
> I walked abroad
> And saw the ruddy moon lean over a hedge
> Like a red-faced farmer.
> I did not stop to speak, but nodded,
> And round about were the wistful stars
> With white faces like town children.

94 Sentence structure

Know the facts

- It is not just the words that writers use that help to make a piece of writing effective. The way in which the words fit together is equally important. The *length* and *type* of sentences used in a text give clues to the overall feel of a piece.

- A **question** or a **command** can make a direct appeal to the reader, or perhaps give the writing a sense of urgency.

> What then must we do? Why, work night and day, body and soul, for the overthrow of the human race! ... Rebellion!
>
> *Animal Farm* by George Orwell

- A **short sentence** can add to the drama and suspense of the text. It can build up the tension, because the full stops on either side mean that there is a longer pause. It can also sound blunt and 'no-nonsense'.

> The telescreen struck fourteen. He must leave in ten minutes. He had to be back at work by fourteen-thirty.
>
> *1984* by George Orwell

- In a **longer sentence**, the pattern of the words can help to give a big picture in one sentence. Here, the long sentence helps suggest a long, hard climb that the party is undertaking.

> At midday, under a pale clear sky, they climbed through a ragged strip of cloud that hung across the peak, well below the shining summits.
>
> *Knowledge of Angels* by Jill Paton Walsh

Test yourself

What is the effect of these two sentences from the World War II poem 'Lessons of the War' by Henry Reed?

1 Today we have naming of parts.

2 Japonica glistens like coral in all of the neighbouring gardens.

Know the facts

It is very difficult to read these two lines aloud as if they were funny:

> His white wet face and miserable eye
> Brought nurses to him more than groans and sighs
>
> 'Died of Wounds' by Siegfried Sassoon

- The tone of the poem ensures that the lines are read in a sombre and cheerless way. The tone a writer gives their writing shows their attitude towards their subject matter and, possibly, to their readers. It helps you work out their mood and feelings.

- A good starting point when identifying the tone of a piece is to imagine reading it aloud. What tone of voice would you use to express its full meaning? Friendly? Humorous? Serious? Sad? Sarcastic?

- In the exam, as well as identifying the tone of a text, you will need to show how you came to your decision. Look at these to help you:
  - the atmosphere (What is the mood or feeling of the piece?)
  - the vocabulary (Does it appeal to your senses? If so, which? In what ways?)
  - sentence structure.

Test yourself

Identify the tone of these two texts.

> (a) Miss J Hunter Dunn, Miss J Hunter Dunn,
> Furnish'd and Burnish'd by Aldershot sun,
> What strenuous singles we played after tea,
> We in the tournament – you against me!
>
> 'A Subaltern's Love-Song' by Sir John Betjeman

> (b) Now is the time for the burning of the leaves.
> They go to the fire; the nostril pricks with smoke
> Wandering slowly into a weeping mist.
>
> 'The Burning of the Leaves' by Laurence Binyon

96 Responding to prose

Know the facts

- When writing about a text it is always necessary to make reference to the text to support the ideas you are putting forward. It is important that you quote the most appropriate words to support your ideas; *don't* just randomly select a quotation!

Look at this section from Frank McCourt's book *Angela's Ashes*:

> Above all – we were wet.
>
> Out in the Atlantic Ocean great sheets of rain gathered to drift slowly up the River Shannon and settle forever in Limerick. The rain dampened the city from the Feast of the Circumcision to New Year's Eve. It created a cacophony of hacking coughs, bronchial rattles, asthmatic wheezes, consumptive croaks. It turned noses into fountains, lungs into bacterial sponges.

- If you were asked in the exam to comment on the author's description of the weather, you might express your ideas like this:

> Frank McCourt wants to emphasise the wet climate of Limerick. He uses words like 'sheets of rain' and 'fountains' to emphasise the amount of water. He also wants us to realise that the climate brought illness, by using words like 'coughs', 'asthmatic' and 'bacterial'.

- The quotations above have been chosen to illustrate the points made in a very focused way. You do not need long quotations; pithy words and phrases are most effective in illustrating your ideas.

Test yourself

Write the next few lines of the commentary on the passage from *Angela's Ashes*.

93
94
95
96

Know the facts

- As poetry uses very precise language, when writing about poetry you often only need to refer to single words. It is usually possible to integrate your references into your sentence so that you can make your points more concisely.

Look at the opening lines of Gillian Clarke's poem 'Miracle on St David's Day':

> An afternoon yellow and open-mouthed
> with daffodils. The sun treads the path
> among cedars and enormous oaks.
> It might be a country house, guests strolling,
> the rumps of gardeners between nursery shrubs.

- If you are asked to write about the setting of the poem, you might write:

> Gillian Clarke tells us about the fine weather on an 'afternoon yellow'. The sun is personified as somebody enjoying a stroll in the garden: he 'treads the path'. This immediately suggests a light, relaxed atmosphere.

The quotations have been included in the flow of the writing to make the points elegantly and lucidly.

Test yourself

Write the next few lines of the commentary on the effect of the setting in 'Miracle on St David's Day'.

Know the facts

- When you are writing about the play you have been studying, you can either quote whole lines of speeches or single words, depending on the point you want to make. To earn maximum marks, you need to explain what makes the scene dramatic.

- In this example from the play *Spring and Port Wine* by Bill Naughton, Betsy Jane, who is careless with money, has come to borrow some money from Mrs Crompton, whose husband insists that their home and finances are run in an orderly fashion.

> **Betsy Jane:** Don't you! Why Mrs Clegg was only saying the other day what she'd do if a man dared attempt to run her side of the home. He might manage to have everything paid up, he might manage to keep the house in order, but in doing so he's sucked all the pride out of you. You talk about not telling him a lie – why, your whole life is a flaming lie if you ask me. How can a man run a home? That's the woman's job – always has been. A man has no right to attempt it. It's not natural.

- If you are asked what this extract shows about Betsy and how it adds to the drama of the scene you might write something like this:

> Betsy is getting annoyed that she can't get the money she desperately needs, so much so that she starts swearing – 'a flaming lie'. She considers looking after money 'her side of the home'. She thinks that Mrs Crompton's life is false: she says that her husband has 'sucked all the pride out' of her, which is a very violent image because it almost suggests he is a vampire.

Test yourself

Write the next few lines of the essay on *Spring and Port Wine*.

99 Comparing texts

Know the facts 📜

- In your coursework you need to include a comparative piece and in the exam you will be asked to compare two poems. It is useful to know the exam board's assessment objectives – you will need to:

- **cross-reference** between the two texts. Remember that 'compare' does not necessarily mean 'find similarities' – significant *differences* are valuable too.

- **understand and evaluate structural and presentational devices.** Basically, this means the writer's choice of *layout* and *structure*. (Look again at sections 67, Rhythm, 68, Rhyme, and 94, Sentence structure, to help you.)

- **understand and evaluate interesting use of language.** Look at the vocabulary chosen and any interesting similes, metaphors and other linguistic devices.

- **develop and sustain interpretation of texts.** In other words, you will need to discuss what the writer wanted to say, what the text *means*. (Look again at sections 92, Atmosphere, and 95, Tone.)

Test yourself 📜

Reread T.E. Hulme's poem 'Autumn' in Unit 93, page 58, Vocabulary, and compare it to the view of Autumn by Keats in Unit 67, page 44, Rhythm.

100 Using cross-references

Know the facts 📜

- When writing about a group of poems, a whole novel or a play you may need to use references from different texts or parts of texts to compare attitudes or ideas in the writing. Sometimes you may be pointing out similarities or, at other times, highlighting difficulties.

- As an example there are several poems by Ted Hughes in which he writes of the power of nature and how people can be overpowered by it. Writing on this topic you could compare the power and effect of the wind in 'Wind' ('This house has been far out at sea all night'; 'we grip our hearts and cannot entertain book, thought, or each other.') with that of the cold winter morning in 'Tractor' ('Hands are like wounds already'; 'Eyes Weeping in the wind of chloroform.'). Here you are cross-referencing quotes from different poems but on a similar theme – the power of nature hurts us at times and we can become frightened by this power. We must accept that the natural world is far stronger than anything we can create.

Test yourself 📜

Read the extracts from Seamus Heaney's poems, 'Follower' in Unit 82, page 51, and 'Digging', below. Put references together from these extracts to show Heaney's admiration for his father.

> Between my finger and my thumb
> The squat pen rests; snug as a gun.
>
> Under my window, a clean rasping sound
> When the spade sinks into gravelly ground:
> My father, digging. I look down.
>
> Till his straining rump among the flowerbeds
> Bends low, comes up twenty years away
> Stooping in rhythm through potato drills
> Where he was digging.
>
> The coarse boot nestled on the lug, the shaft
> Against the inside knee was levered firmly.
> He rooted out tall tops, buried the bright edge deep
> To scatter new potatoes that we picked
> Loving their cool hardness in our hands.
>
> By God, the old man could handle a spade.
> Just like his old man.

Answers

02 Spelling simple words

interest, business, already, friends, different, clothes, a lot

03 Prefixes and suffixes

Here are some possible answers, but there are others:

1 <u>mis</u>carry, <u>dis</u>connect, <u>in</u>dependent, <u>in</u>direct, <u>un</u>helpful, <u>un</u>kind, <u>im</u>mature or <u>pre</u>mature, <u>im</u>pulse, <u>in</u>sincere

2 expect<u>ant</u>, general<u>ly</u>, grace<u>fully</u>, move<u>ment</u>, perform<u>ance</u>, persist<u>ent</u>, point<u>less</u>, short<u>ness</u>, thank<u>fully</u>, walk<u>ing</u>

04 What is punctuation?

1 (a) exclamation mark
  (b) comma
  (c) full stop
  (d) capital letter
  (e) question mark

2 Have you understood this page so far? Just to recap, if you don't use punctuation then your words become very difficult to follow. The reader becomes confused and your writing becomes less effective. You must punctuate your writing if you want your reader to understand what you have written. Simple!

05 Useful spelling rules

1 bikes, cars, lives, men, babies, boxes, families, princesses, stitches, thieves, sheep, matches

2 hurried, tipped, cried, laughed, called, hated, pushed, emptied, spotted, lied, stopped, fried

06 Further punctuation

The children's father walked slowly along the beach. He didn't want to give up the search just yet. On the horizon the sun was closing over the water's edge; the day was almost ended. As he walked he thought of all the things that had gone wrong over the past week: the lost luggage, the dirty hotel room, the rain and now this. His thoughts were disturbed by shouts in the distance.

'Over here. There's something over here.'

Now he was running; running in the direction of the voices.

08 Adjectives

silent, vicious, drawn, spiteful, invisible, cruel, more important

10 Adverbs

lazily, gently, silently, forwards

coldly, dangerously, mischievously, mysteriously, restlessly, thoughtfully, quickly, angrily

12 Types of sentence structures

The room was full. (simple) Inside, bodies heaved and shook to the sound of the music. (complex) Nobody heard the boy as he entered the room. (compound) Nobody saw him until it was too late. (compound)

1 Here is one possible example: The children, their coats and bags trailing behind them, ran excitedly, and with loud shouts of joy, through the wrought iron school gates.

13 Thinking about sentence forms

Kathy left school immediately after her GCSEs. She had no job to go to but at first she wasn't too worried. She had her brains, her confidence and three hundred pounds in her pocket. (group of three) Why should she worry? (rhetorical question) Two months later she wasn't so confident; two months later (repetition) she still had her brains but her money had disappeared along with her confidence. She didn't know which way to turn. She was frightened. (short sentence)

15 Dealing with tenses

present: I talk, I am talking

past: I talked, I have talked, I had talked, I was talking

future: I will be talking, I shall talk, I will talk, I will have talked.

17 Writing for purpose

(a) to inform the public and to persuade them to buy the product
(b) to argue your point of view
(c) to describe the experiment, analyse and explain the results
(d) to inform the governors and to promote Year 11

23 Setting

Make a list of everything you are told, for instance, in the first paragraph: no rain, sun compared to a yellow furnace, dry streams and parched earth.

38 Writing reports

Who? Fifa   What? In confusion   Where? Contest to hold the 2006 World Cup When? Yesterday   Why? Death threat How? Made against one of its members.

41 Setting out a letter

(a) Write a formal letter. Use the layout shown at the start of this Unit.
(b) Write an informal letter. Follow the advice on informal letters in this Unit.

43 Thinking about the question

Q1 a letter

Q2 to persuade readers that punishment today is not harsh enough

Q3 local newspaper readers

Q4 writing to persuade

48 Checking your work

When I got home I sat and cried. I couldn't work out what I had done that was supposed to be so bad. I was shaking and had a bad headache so I went to bed early. I didn't want my mum to know what had happened as it would upset her. Once I got to bed I stopped shaking and started to feel calmer, though it was a long time before I got to sleep.

49 Checking your work

Here's an example of the kind of redrafting you might do to this paragraph. When I arrived home I simply sat and cried. What had I done that was supposed to be so terrible? I was shaking and my head ached so I went to bed early. I didn't want mum to know what had happened; it would only upset her. Once I lay down I started to feel more calm, though it was many hours before I drifted into an unsettled sleep.

51 Audience

1 (a) a movie-fan (with a video at home!)
  (b) a health-conscious person
  (c) somebody who wanted a quick grasp of the headlines

52 Purpose

1 (a) to advertise a video store
  (b) to promote the healthy qualities of the product
  (c) to give a brief impression of the day's main news and help sell the paper

53 Identifying facts

1 fact   2 fact   3 not a fact
4 fact

54 Identifying opinions

1 opinion   2 fact   3 opinion
4 opinion

57 Bias

Only one point of view is shown – the speaker doesn't seem to consider other viewpoints. There are no facts to back up his/her opinions. He/she seems to be trying to influence the audience.

58 Recognising inconsistencies

The passage begins by making the point that being seriously underweight is a health problem. It goes on to suggest that living on foods such as burgers, chips and chocolates will solve this problem. This is inconsistent because, while it could be true that teenagers would no longer be underweight, it would certainly not cure their health problems — they could be seriously overweight and badly nourished.

63 Persuasive writing

(a) direct address, group of three

(b) balanced sentence

(c) direct appeal

65 Selecting material appropriate to purpose

Your answers might include:

Front page of a tabloid newspaper — big, bold headline to grab attention, large photograph featuring people (famous, if possible), very little text at a smaller size.

Front page of a quality newspaper — headline (but smaller than the tabloid); several columns of smaller text, with subheadings; one large photo (but not as large as the tabloid); a few smaller photos; list of what else is in the newspaper.

Letters page of a teenage magazine — photo of editor; photos of some of the letter-writers; headline highlighting a featured letter; different typefaces to suggest the different writers and for the magazine's responses to the letters; informal language to show that the editor 'speaks their language'; special features, such as a joke of the week or 'most embarrassing story'.

Flyer for new video rental outlet — eye-catching design; big headline type; possibly bright colours, star-shaped boxes and exclamation marks to emphasise messages, such as 'New!', 'Great value!' etc.; details of location and prices; pictures of some recent, popular videos.

Page in a dictionary — fairly small, dense text; use of bold and italic type for different types of information; pages may be set in more than one column of text; abbreviations used, such as (n) for noun; no illustrations, unless it is an illustrated dictionary.

67 Rhythm

1   <u>Half</u> a league, <u>half</u> a league, <u>half</u> a league onward
    The rhythm imitates horses' hooves galloping into battle.

2   <u>Up</u> and <u>down</u>, <u>up</u> and <u>down</u>,
    They <u>go</u>, the <u>gray</u> rat, <u>and</u> the brown.
    The quick, upbeat rhythm creates a sense of urgency.

68 Rhyme

The soft rhymes give a sense of calmness and peace, highly appropriate for a cemetery. The rhymes give the poem a gentle, flowing musical quality that suits the mood. The rhymes help us remember the poem, and accordingly remember the men who died.

70 Metaphors

Simile: 'like a roll of foil'

Metaphor: 'The rain is a recorder'

The writer is asking you to imagine a drive through the rain.

The simile 'like a roll of foil' effectively suggests the wet road glistening in the headlights. It is shiny and leads off into the distance like an unrolled roll of silver foil.

The metaphor 'The rain is a recorder' cleverly suggests both the look and the sound of the rain. The noise of raindrops is like a tune the rain is writing and the raindrops look like musical notes on the telegraph wires. Droplets running down the kerbs and cats' eyes could also look like writing.

72 Alliteration

1   'tinkling trees', 'weeping willows'

2   The short *t* sounds help to suggest the sound of the icy trees when the branches tap against each other (like the tinkling of glass). The *w* sounds are longer and more mournful, reflecting the heaviness of the icy branches.

73 Assonance, consonance and sibilance

1   The consonance helps to suggest the weariness of the journey. The *g* sounds are heavy and plodding.

2   The sibilance helps to suggest the sound of the bullets whistling through the air.

74 Onomatopoeia

The onomatopoeic words are *cracks*, *snapping* and *coughs*.

75 Hyperbole

1   'an ocean' – there may be a lot of water, but not as much as an ocean.

2   The idea that an ocean comes pouring out of the guttering stresses the huge volume of water involved. This makes the gargoyles themselves more frightening – they appear powerful enough to have swallowed a whole ocean.

76 Repetition

The emphasis on red creates a frightening impression. We imagine the room to be red, dark and overpowering.

77 Irony

This is ironic because the man mistook Pip's answer to mean that his mother was nearby, when in fact she was dead and buried. The passage is comic but poignant too.

78 Dramatic irony

The audience knows that World War One broke out in 1914 and that the Titanic sank, proving Mr Birling wrong. This makes the audience wonder whether his other judgements in the play may be equally mistaken. It also gives a sense of gloom, as his optimism proved unfounded.

79 Narrators

(a) first   (b) third

80 Prose: character

She brought with her, two <u>uncompromising</u> <u>hard</u> <u>black</u> boxes, with her initials on the lids in <u>hard</u> <u>brass</u> <u>nails</u>. When she paid the coachman she took her money out of a <u>hard</u> <u>steel</u> purse, and she kept the purse in a very <u>jail</u> of a bag which hung upon her arm by a <u>heavy chain</u>, and shut up like a <u>bite</u>. I had never, at that time, seen such a <u>metallic</u> lady altogether as Miss Murdstone was.

81 Prose: setting

<u>Fog</u> everywhere. <u>Fog</u> up the river, where it flows among green aits and meadows; <u>fog</u> down the river, where it rolls <u>defiled</u> among the tiers of shipping, and the waterside <u>pollutions</u> of a great (and <u>dirty</u>) city. The <u>raw</u> afternoon is <u>rawest</u>, and the <u>dense</u> fog is <u>densest</u>, and the <u>muddy</u> streets are <u>muddiest</u>, near ... Temple Bar.

The underlined words give an impression of savagery and evil. Dickens goes on to describe dirt and noise. He was trying to convey his feeling that industrialisation in the Industrial Revolution led to decay in people's lives. The language helps you to engage with his message.

82 Poetry: character

The following is an example answer.

Owen has used similes to create a clear picture of exhaustion. Young men, who should be fit and well, are seen as bent as old beggars. They are coughing like old women.

(Look at section 69, Similes, for more information on the technique Owen uses here.)

83 Poetry: setting

The land's sharp features seemed to be
The Century's <u>corpse</u> outleant,
His <u>crypt</u> the cloudy canopy
The wind his <u>death</u> <u>lament</u>,
The <u>ancient pulse</u> of germ and birth

Was <u>shrunken</u> <u>hard</u> <u>and</u> <u>dry</u>,
And every spirit upon earth
Seemed <u>fervourless</u> as I.

84 Drama: character 1

The extract shows Barbara is determined, tough and encouraging to her friend who needs support.

85 Drama: character 2

Willy Loman shows signs of exhaustion from overwork; he is an average sort of person, who never did anything to mark him out; he has a wife who is concerned about him.

86 Drama: setting

The description of the setting tells us that it is a rural community and that the atmosphere is calm and peaceful.

87 Shakespeare: blank verse

1 true **2**   true   **3**   false

89 Shakespeare: prose

He is (too) fond of drink.

He may be a military man (he refers to his boots).

He can be violent (he talks of hanging quite freely).

He is confident and brash.

90 Dialect

1 Explain to me what exactly you mean when you say 'half-caste'. Do you mean that when Picasso mixed red and green he created a half-caste canvas?

2 The poet is angry that people of mixed race are often victims of racial prejudice. He points out that some of the most wonderful things ever created were made by mixing colours, such as Picasso's paintings. Therefore, a person of mixed race should be seen as equally wonderful, not someone to be prejudiced against.

91 Cultural aspects

1 When water catches the light it appears to be a silvery colour. More importantly, silver is something very precious, just as water is precious to the people in the poem.

2 The water gushes out of the pipe in a roar. Also, the news of the leak spreads quickly in the community – tongues roar out the good news of the unexpected flow of water.

93 Vocabulary: the five senses

A <u>touch</u> <u>of</u> <u>cold</u> in the Autumn night – **touch**

I walked abroad

And <u>saw</u> <u>the</u> <u>ruddy</u> <u>moon</u> lean over a hedge
         sight

Like a <u>red-faced</u> farmer.   **sight**

I <u>did</u> <u>not</u> <u>stop</u> <u>to</u> <u>speak</u>, but nodded,   **sound**

And round about were the wistful stars

With <u>white</u> <u>faces</u> like town children. **sight**

94 Sentence structure

1 short, abrupt sentence – like a military order

2 long, flowing sentence helps the reader to picture the relaxed scene

95 Tone

(a) amusing, light-hearted

(b) reflective, mournful, thoughtful

96 Responding to prose

The following is an example answer.

McCourt has made very effective use of **onomatopoeia** so that we can <u>hear</u> the unpleasant 'cacophony of coughs', 'rattles' and 'wheezes' that the weather produces (particularly with the cough-like **alliteration**). The Feast of the Circumcision is January 1st, so the fact that the wet weather lasts from then until New Year's Eve stresses that the dampness was almost permanent.

97 Responding to poetry

The following is an example answer.

The trees, 'cedars and enormous oaks', are very imposing and suggest a grandeur about the garden. The poet tells us the place was like a 'country house' with 'guests' and 'gardeners', although there is a hint of humour in the way that we can only see the 'rumps' of the gardeners as they bend over their work.

98 Responding to drama

The following is an example answer.

Betsy Jane's rhetorical question 'How can a man run a home?' emphasises that she thinks that it is 'not natural'. Her short sentences at the end show how definite she is and that she wants her argument to hit home.

99 Comparing texts

The following is an example answer.

* structural and presentational devices – both use flowing sentences to give a calm, restful atmosphere.

* understand and evaluate interesting use of language – both use personification, but Hulme personifies the moon almost humorously while Keats personifies Autumn itself as a friend.

* develop and sustain interpretation of texts – both see Autumn as a soft, gentle time.

100 Using cross-references

'Follower': 'An expert' and 'The sod rolled over without breaking' show his skill; 'Mapping the furrow exactly' indicates his expertise.

'Digging': 'the shaft ... was levered firmly' shows his skill; 'By God, the old man could handle a spade' is clear praise.

Acknowledgements

Every effort has been made to trace the copyright holders of the material in this book. If, however, any omissions have been made, we would be happy to rectify this. Please contact us at the address on the title page.

'End of days' review, by permission of *More* June 14-27, 2000; Article: Ministers plan 50% increase in adoptions, The Guardian 8/7/2000 by permission of Guardian and Observer Syndication; *A Drink of Water* by kind permission of Althea Selvon, wife of Samuel Selvon; Debate: Match of the Day, Manchester Evening News, 15/6/2000 by permission of the Manchester Evening News; Article: House prices begin to slide, The Guardian 8/7/2000 by permission of Guardian and Observer

Syndication; Review: 'A Life Less Ordinary', *TV Quick* 23-29 Sep 2000; 'Valentine', by kind permission of Anvil Press Poetry Ltd. on behalf of Carol Ann Duffy; Principal Examiners' Report; 'In memory of W.B Yeats' by W.H. Auden courtesy of Curtis Brown; 'Poem' by Simon Armiatge, taken from *Kids* by permission of Faber and Faber Ltd.; 'Wind', 'Tractor' from *Moortown* by Ted Hughes, by permission of Faber and Faber Ltd ; 'The Sea' by permission of Laura Cecil on behalf of James Reeves; 'Miracle on St David's Day' and 'Nightride' by Gillian Clarke by permission of Carcanet Press; 'Hard Frost' by Rev. Andrew Young by permission of Carcanet New Press; 'Ile de la Cite' ©Jim McRae; 'First Ice' by Andre Voznesensky by permission of

Random House UK Ltd.; 'Follower' and 'Digging' by Seamus Heaney by permission of Faber and Faber Ltd.; 'Unrelated Incidents' by Tom Leonard, permission of Tom Leonard; 'Half Caste' John Agard by permission of Caroline Sheldon Literary Agency; 'Old Father' ©Hugh Boatswain; 'Blessing' ©Imtiaz Dharker; 'Died of Wounds' by Siegfried Sassoon by permission of George Sassoon; 'A Subaltern's Love-Song' by Sir John Betjeman by permission of John Murray Publishers Ltd.; 'The Burning of the Leaves' by Laurence Binyon by permission of The Society of Authors.